The Art of Scenic Design

INTRODUCTIONS TO THEATRE

SERIES EDITOR:
JIM VOLZ, CALIFORNIA STATE UNIVERSITY, FULLERTON, USA

This series of textbooks provides a practical introduction to core areas of theatre and performance, and has been designed to support semester teaching plans. Each book offers case studies and international examples of practice, and will equip undergraduate students and emerging theatre professionals with the understanding and skills necessary to succeed—whether in study or in the entertainment industry.

Directing Professionally: A Practical Guide to Developing a Successful Career in Today's Theatre
Kent Thompson
ISBN 978-1-4742-8876-7

Get the Job in the Entertainment Industry: A Practical Guide for Designers, Technicians, and Stage Managers
Kristina Tollefson
ISBN 978-1-3501-0378-8

Introduction to the Art of Stage Management: A Practical Guide to Working in the Theatre and Beyond
Michael Vitale
ISBN 978-1-4742-5720-6

Introduction to Arts Management
Jim Volz
ISBN 978-1-4742-3978-3

The Art of Writing for the Theatre: An Introduction to Script Analysis, Criticism and Playwriting
Luke Yankee
ISBN 978-1-3501-5557-2

The Art of Scenic Design

A Practical Guide to the Creative Process

Robert Mark Morgan

methuen | drama
LONDON • NEW YORK • OXFORD • NEW DELHI • SYDNEY

METHUEN DRAMA
Bloomsbury Publishing Plc
50 Bedford Square, London, WC1B 3DP, UK
1385 Broadway, New York, NY 10018, USA
29 Earlsfort Terrace, Dublin 2, Ireland

BLOOMSBURY, METHUEN DRAMA and the Methuen Drama logo are trademarks of Bloomsbury Publishing Plc

First published in Great Britain 2022

Copyright © Robert Mark Morgan, 2022

Robert Mark Morgan has asserted his right under the Copyright, Designs and Patents Act, 1988, to be identified as Author of this work.

For legal purposes the Acknowledgments on p. xiv constitute an extension of this copyright page.

Cover design by www.ironicitalics.com
Cover image © *The Moon for the Misbegotten* at the American Conservatory Theatre, San Francisco.
Set design and photo by Robert Mark Morgan.

All rights reserved. No part of this publication may be reproduced or transmitted in any form or by any means, electronic or mechanical, including photocopying, recording, or any information storage or retrieval system, without prior permission in writing from the publishers.

Bloomsbury Publishing Plc does not have any control over, or responsibility for, any third-party websites referred to or in this book. All internet addresses given in this book were correct at the time of going to press. The author and publisher regret any inconvenience caused if addresses have changed or sites have ceased to exist, but can accept no responsibility for any such changes.

A catalogue record for this book is available from the British Library.

A catalog record for this book is available from the Library of Congress.

ISBN: HB: 978-1-3501-3955-8
PB: 978-1-3501-3954-1
ePDF: 978-1-3501-3957-2
eBook: 978-1-3501-3956-5

Series: Introductions to Theatre

Typeset by RefineCatch Limited, Bungay, Suffolk
Printed and bound in India

To find out more about our authors and books visit www.bloomsbury.com and sign up for our newsletters.

To my parents
who taught me both the power of
big dreams
and
small gestures
of kindness

Contents

Illustrations

Figures

Plates

Foreword

There are many fine textbooks that describe the step-by-step process of designing a set for a live theatre production, and the set designer's responsibilities. They show how to draw perspective sketches of your ideas, translate those sketches into scale models, drafted elevations of the scenery, and methods to build, paint, decorate and automate that set.

Unfortunately, most of these books now need to be updated every few years because the methods that set designers once employed to approach, visualize, and ultimately communicate these design ideas to others began to change in the 1990s when the personal computer started to become an important tool in the stage-design process. Now, the computers become more powerful every year, and the programs used in stage design are developed, improved, and upgraded so often that we buy subscriptions to this software, so that it can update itself monthly. Today it is possible to create a computer image of a set design that, to the untrained eye, looks like a photograph of a fully realized production. Tomorrow ... who knows? It can all be a bit overwhelming.

We must also realize that, at this point in time, no computer program can decide what your actual set *should* be.

Where *do* you start? Where do your ideas come from?

That is what this book is about.

Robert Mark Morgan is an award-winning professional set designer employed by many of the top theatres in the country. He has been involved in the education of theatre design undergraduate and graduate students since 2003. He also has an absolute belief in the inherent creative spirit residing in everyone. It is the fundamental idea behind this book.

Mr Morgan discusses how a young theatre artist can use their innate creative intelligence to collaborate with a script, a director, and other designers to shape an idea that grows from their own collective experiences into the design for a play. But how do we access that information in ourselves? How do we find the confidence to believe in our ideas and overcome the natural fear of being vulnerable? You do not really teach these things any more than you teach someone to breath or see, but there are methods and training that can focus these natural acts for a purpose.

This book unfolds like a one-on-one class with a with a very knowledgeable, entertaining, professor. Robert's belief in the power of the theatre and its value to our society is inspiring and his examples, drawn from his own career, illuminate his ideas. He presents the "What Ifs," the possibilities, and the joy of designing for the theatre. This is a book aimed at starting out design students, but I think it is very valuable to all theatre artists of any age or experience. To be clearly reminded of how and why we design for the theatre is always a worthwhile, refreshing experience.

Ralph Funicello
Powell Chair in Set Design, San Diego State University
Associate Artist, Old Globe Theatre

Acknowledgments

My wife, Rebecca Jaynes Morgan, who has supported me in this and so many other dreams.

Holly Gabelmann and her love of formatting and all things mind-numbing to me. Without her, this book would not exist.

Ralph Funicello who made hope visible for me and influenced me as a designer, educator, and man.

Jim Volz who thought I could write this book when I did not think I could . . . or should.

Mark Dudgeon who provided valuable wisdom along the way.

Ella Wilson who has been patient with all my stupid questions and crazy ideas.

Paula Devine for her editing prowess and patience.

Merv Honeywood and Megan Jones who made sure this text looks beautifully polished and produced.

The author and publisher gratefully acknowledge the permission granted to reproduce the copyright material in this book

Every effort has been made to trace copyright holders and to obtain their permission for the use of copyright material. However, if any have been inadvertently overlooked, the publishers will be pleased, if notified of any omissions, to make the necessary arrangement at the first opportunity.

The third party copyrighted material displayed in the pages of this book are done so on the basis of "fair dealing for the purposes of criticism and review" or "fair use for the purposes of teaching, criticism, scholarship or research" only in accordance with international copyright laws, and is not intended to infringe upon the ownership rights of the original owners.

Introduction: . . . "And Just Like That"

Chapter Outline

The Theatrical Identity Crisis—and the Opportunities it Presents

It is safe to say that the art of entertainment was cruising along in early 2020. Institutional norms were . . . normal. Tickets across the spectrum of offerings from Broadway to concerts to small local theatres were selling as they always had been. Seasons were being planned. Designs were being submitted. Scripts were being written.

And *just. like. that.*

Mother Nature shrugged and reminded us of her power to force change upon us. Before long, animals of all kinds were seen strolling city streets and reclaiming territory that was once their domain while we, as humans, pondered this tremendous collective experience that forced us to recognize our vulnerability, our hubris, and our folly. To say that we have had a sea change is to assume that the change only affects the sea. Why not also the land? Societies? Regimes?

The theatre and, in fact, the entire entertainment world underwent a transformation prompted by a virus, but in hindsight may be considered a worthwhile and prescient "pause" to reflect on what we do in the theatre, how we do it, who we do it with, and what stories are we telling with it. Are traditional lessons in any artform that involves the gathering of souls and the sharing of stories valid any longer? What brushstrokes of color from that former painting are relevant to this new and uncertain one? I write this to you as an author who crafted a portion of this book from what seems to be a different time and seemingly a different world entirely at least from a theatrical and systemic structure point of view. The world seems to have been altered somehow, like a blank canvas awaiting a new first brushstroke of paint. But what color? What brush? And should we be even creating a painting at all? Is an abundance of clay and patience a more suitable medium for our next steps?

Or perhaps a better analogy is a puzzle: picture a table on which sits a puzzle of the entire world—like "Risk" but without the armies. The table and therefore the entire puzzle has been thrown into the air. We stand at the precipice of a moment when we can place those pieces, not back to where they were, but to a different location entirely.

> We tell ourselves stories in order to live ... We look for the sermon in the suicide, for the social or moral lesson in the murder of five. We interpret what we see, select the most workable of the multiple choices.[1]
>
> Joan Didion

Rely on Story—Always

Stories are what make us human. Others may disagree but, in my humble opinion, storytelling is a basic human need as essential as air and water. Humans are social animals. There is a real human need to connect by story with another human. A tale well told helps remind us both *why* we are human and *that* we are human. It allows us to imagine new worlds better than our current one and gives us a moment in time to float to another time and place. Since the first Dr Seuss book a parent may have read to you as a child, it has been clear that storytelling is more of a need than a want, whether it be the one-on-one venue of story commonplace at your local coffee shop or a voyeuristic story we see onstage before us in a play. We NEED a good story!

> Every great design begins with an even better story.
>
> Lorinda Mamo, designer[2]

In a "new normal," HOW we do that storytelling moving forward can—and perhaps should—be something entirely different from this point and into the future. For a book about "design," it seems important to point out that the system that supported big-budget theatre, before the shake up, was not broken. It was working *by design*. That *design* largely meant a prioritization of the work of theatre and the arts as a means-to-an-end which satisfies the shareholders and corporate sponsors. In some (not all) cases theatre catered to the siren song of financial success and Times Square-scale marketing to the theatre consumer. The "product" was theatre and the goal was (and perhaps still is) success defined by corporate sponsors and marketing schemes. "Butts in seats" was the goal always.

As a child, my parents did me a huge favor without even knowing it. In those days, my friends were playing with officially trademarked Lego sets with the best visual packaging that could be designed illustrating what you could make with what was in that magical box: spaceships and Star Wars sets, entire cities, and fancy cars. Each box had a sort of pre-destined outcome: a prescription for what you were supposed to do with the loose pieces and parts. At the time, it seemed remarkably exciting to be able to get one of those sets of Legos and make exactly what you were *supposed* to make with it. That was the prescription. My parents were more frugal and we tended to buy the department store brand of items that were honestly the same quality, but for a much better price. You were not "paying for the name" as I recall my mother saying. I got the 5-gallon bucket of "Brix Blox" made by Sears. It was a giant bucket of Legos. That was it. No frills. Just make stuff with it. And I did. I would dump out the entire 1,400-piece bucket, mutter something to myself "I'm going to make a doghouse" or whatever and just start clicking pieces together. I would make something, share it with whomever had the fortitude to listen to me explain it, and eventually bust it up, put it in the bucket, and start the whole process over another time.

Renowned architect Frank Gehry references a similar experience in a documentary about his life:

> I remember ... I must have been about eight years old. My grandmother used to get a sack full of wood cuttings for the wood stove. Every once in a while, she'd open the sack and throw the stuff out on the floor and sit down on the floor with me and start building things. We made cities and freeways. It was so much fun! I remember when I was struggling: What do want to be when you grow up? Somehow, I kept remembering sitting on the floor with the blocks. Intuitively I thought: maybe I could do something like that?
>
> Frank Gehry, *The Sketches of Frank Gehry*, directed by Sydney Pollack[3]

I relate these stories as a means of conveying where we are at this moment in artistic history. We have had the bucket dumped. The blocks are on the floor. Random. Scattered. But ripe with possibility and reformation in a new way. A more equitable way. To paraphrase Benjamin Franklin, a new republic of theatre . . . if we can keep it.

> You never change things by fighting against the existing reality. To change something, build a new model that makes the old model obsolete.
>
> Buckminster Fuller[4]

A puzzle thrown into the air represents a possibility that had not previously existed. Accolades and artistic recognition for Renaissance artists did, at one time, typically center around an artist's ability to capture a moment in time to a supremely accurate level of authenticity bordering on photorealistic. The brow of a subject furrowed just so. The positioned hand of the subject. The artist's hand so delicately and carefully manipulated the paint to portray reality—or at least a glowing version of reality. Later, and with the very same paint and colors, new art forms emerged from artists like Jackson Pollack and Vasily Kandinsky. The paint could be arranged in a new way to make a new meaning and new purpose for the genre. It was no longer delicately placed and pre-mixed. Artists now chose to attack a canvas rather than pamper it. Artists felt the medium could better convey emotion—and meaning—and purpose—not from a subtle touch, but from an aggressive movement. Again: same paint, same brushes, radically different results.

We seem to be at *that* point (whether we like it or not) right now. A shift in our art form that represents possibility and potential more than it reflects on the past. We are and may continue to be for many years to come, in a liminal space that began with the destruction of all of our collective normal and now moves us to craft a new norm in the absence of the old one.

> A disaster produces chaos immediately, but the people hit by that chaos usually improvise a fleeting order that is more like . . . mutual-aid societies than it is like the society that existed before the explosion or earthquake or fire. It liberates people to revert to a latent sense of self and principle, one more generous, braver, and more resourceful than we ordinarily see.
>
> Rebecca Solnit[5]

We are in a situation where we need to similarly "improvise a fleeting order" and reinvent—or at least refocus—our art form as we might post-disaster. We are all in uncharted—dare I say "exciting"—territory here on a ship destined for a new age of storytelling in perhaps new spaces and into new realms of possibility. Change is coming. Choose whatever analogy you desire, but the undeniable truth we must take at face value is that we simply cannot (nor should we) return to normal in any field. We have been afforded a pause from the race we imposed upon ourselves when theatre was thriving. We must accept that pause as a means to recharge and reflect on what we do as artists beginning with *why* we do it in the first place.

Adjacent Possible and the Liminal Space

In the design world, there exists a simple concept called the "adjacent possible." It essentially means that two paths of sometimes entirely unrelated advancements in separate fields beget new innovations when those two paths reach a certain level. Take glass for example. The island of Murano, Italy is widely considered to be the birthplace of glass. On that island, glassmakers have been learning from each other and manufacturing glass for the better part of 700 years since the thirteenth century. But consider what happens when experimentation in that medium leads to a discovery that curved pieces of glass can be placed over our eyes allowing us to see better? More people can read! That begets advancements that lead to the printing press and a complete revolution in the consumption of information which has accelerated ever since. Now that everyone can read their news (because they can *see* it), they do not need it read aloud to them. And what happens when you line up a pair of convex lenses in sequence? Now we have moved to studying the stars and seeing great distances in addition to very close up. Voila! The adjacent possible.

As the properties of glass led to innovations and new uses of it, the elimination of a key element to theatrical storytelling can lead to a profound and real-time thought experiment: How do we do what we do without the space we do it in? More importantly, what opportunities does that provide us? If constraint is a catalyst for creativity, what do we make now—and why—and *where*?

Combine an earthshattering and resonant call for equity and a common humanity across all aspects of our society with new technologies and tools that democratize the artmaking so anyone can be a storyteller and can share that story with the world in a click and we are at a theatrical adjacent possible. Before this shift, reward drove performance. Big shows at big theatres made big money. Touring companies reaped the rewards of a good Broadway run and multiple tours would be launched to maximize profits across the board for all. Theatre was, and always has been I suppose, a machine. To tell stories and make money off that storytelling. We are at a place now where it is not reward, but *purpose* that must drive performance. The house has fallen down all around us, and it is storytelling that remains in the middle unscathed. We start there. With *story*.

> Artists without galleries, designers without clients, actors without audiences—we are all paddling our own canoes, now. To invent new equations for ourselves in the uncertainty of so much radical vulnerability is terrifying. It is unprecedented. It is profoundly isolating.
>
> Jessica Helfand, Editor of Design Observer[6]

What has Changed . . . and What has Not

Perhaps we may take comfort in the knowledge that theatre as a craft has somehow managed to endure the epic passage of time since the Festival of Dionysus was first trumpeted into existence in 476 B.C. As an art form, it has been viewed in different ways by different people of different faiths and tremendously different extremes. Theatre has been both vilified and utilized for centuries and has for generations served as both the scapegoat and the savior. It has been characterized as both a sacrilegious corruptor of souls and a vehicle for spreading the word of God Himself through the power of the spoken word story brought to the masses of people who needed to *hear* the "word of God" . . . because they could not *read* it. But this moment in time is a moment where we must reach back and look forward simultaneously.

Case in point:

In the Middle Ages, the word of God was spread to both the faithful and the faithless via what was known as a pageant wagon. This (literal) vehicle made mobile stories of moral choices and accentuated the polarity of heaven and hell, so all audiences knew the choices faced and the fate tempted for choices made that did not comply with God's will.

But when a virus shuts down indoor venues worldwide, artists do not—and should not—stop working. Look at my design for a twenty-first century version of a fifteenth-century pageant wagon.

If public health codes and university rules prohibit indoor gatherings to see work onstage? Fine! Let us move the stage outdoors, shall we? A few

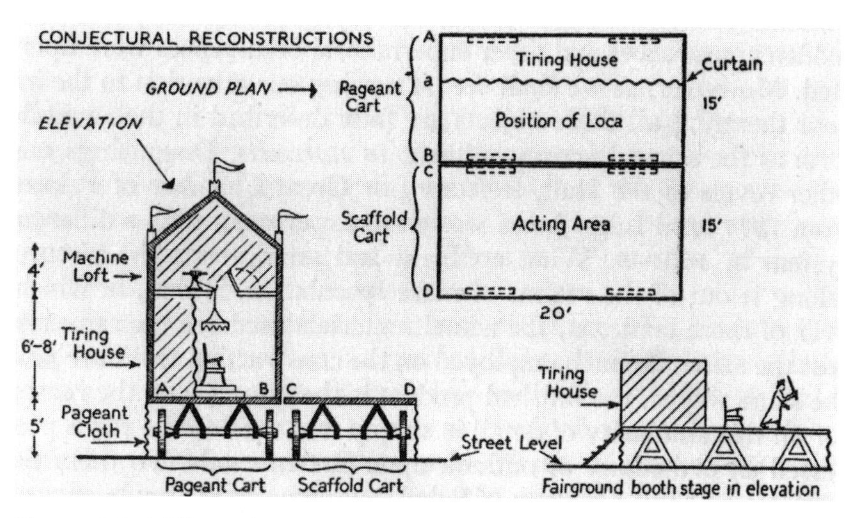

Figure 0.1 A Fifteenth-century Pageant Wagon. *Source: Wickham,* Early English Stages, *Vol I., University of Bristol/ArenaPAL.*

Figure 0.2 A Twenty-first Century Pageant Wagon (design by Robert Mark Morgan). *Source: design by author.*

walls, speakers, stairs, and some lights mounted to a utility trailer and pulled around campus is what you see in our eagerly anticipated drama department pageant wagon. Complete with a small window for puppet shows out the back, the unit is as flexible as it is festive.

For reasons scholars will continue to debate, the flame of the theatrical art form has been reduced to a flicker, but thankfully, has never been extinguished. Steinbeck may have put it best when he wrote:

> The theatre is the only institution in the world that has been dying for four thousand years and has never succumbed. It requires tough and devoted people to keep it alive.
>
> John Steinbeck, author[7]

Perhaps an audience will always exist for those who wish to take a ride on the theme park ride for the soul, but I think that perhaps the reason may be a shade more profound.

With history on our side, we must do what designers do! We must see a future that does not exist ... *yet*. We must ask of ourselves what we ask of our patrons. When lost in the woods, what do we do to find our way out? We become hyper-aware of our surroundings. We sense the sound of water nearby or the trajectory of the sun as it crosses the sky or the existence of any evidence whatsoever of human interaction with that environment. Anywhere and everywhere, we look—with extreme awareness and sensitivity—for clues about where we go next. That is where we are now. At this moment. At this juncture in the history of the planet and the societies that have existed on that planet since two or more people began to gather. We are in a liminal space and one which can (and has) produced equal parts fear and anticipation for what comes next. Liminal: crossing lintels or thresholds. That is where we are right now. Living with uncertainty.

I am also reminded that certain principles remain unchanged in the profession. The concept of hard work, long hours of dedication, and being kind and courteous to those artists you work alongside (although perhaps more "socially distanced" now) are as useful post pandemic as they were pre pandemic. Seems best to start there and see where the journey takes us. After all, that is why we were drawn to the theatre in the first place, right? We like going on a journey with a completely ambiguous outcome in the hands of expert storytellers and in a space crafted by fine designers specifically *for that story*. We are living our own unknown-ending play right now as human beings with roles for virtually everyone from artists and designers to engineers and scientists. So together: let us figure out the way forward.

Set in the context of my own story as a theatrical set designer, this book attempts to unpack and demystify what it truly means to be a theatre designer in the twenty-first century beyond and beneath the technical skills necessary to do so. Designers need to be good collaborators and proficient idea generators. They need to dedicate themselves to the process of crafting and telling a story with other collaborators in a way that supports and uplifts *that* production at *this* time and for *this particular* audience. Each production is a new process unique to that creative process at that time and with those specific collaborators. When it works, there is no greater feeling in the world to have participated in and shared that experience with other artists. This book is meant to bring out and highlight the key ingredients that make a theatrical recipe "work" for a modern audience in a way (we hope) that profoundly affects them and changes the way they see their world differently when they exit the theatre than they did when they entered. I invite you to come along with me as I share theatre stories and lessons applicable to anyone who strives to explore creativity through a theatrical lens. I hope you enjoy the view.

1

The Designer as A Child Futurist

Chapter Outline

Who I am and Why you Should Bother to Care

In 1992, Admiral James Stockdale spoke at a podium during a Vice-Presidential debate alongside Al Gore and Dan Quayle. Admiral Stockdale was there representing himself as the running mate to then candidate H. Ross Perot for the Presidency of the United States. Admiral Stockdale and Perot were outsiders and represented what was, at that time, an unheard of run at the Presidency from a third-party candidate. Admiral Stockdale was a highly decorated war veteran and, with a full head of gray hair, even *looked* out of place alongside the younger, taller, and arguably more handsome pair of Gore and Quayle. As is customary, all three vice presidential candidates got an opportunity to make an opening statement to the audience and made their case for the highest office in the land in what has been deemed the most powerful country on the planet. Admiral Stockdale began his opening remarks for this esteemed, respected, and powerful office with, by contrast, seven simple words that secured his place in political lore for decades to come: "Who am I? Why am I here?"

It is with these seven words in mind that I would like to introduce myself to you, the reader. I'd like you to know the answers to the questions that Admiral Stockdale posed in 1992 as well as the answer to another significant question that I hope to answer: "Why should I read this book?"

Who am I?

By my own and the accounts of many of my peers, I have thoroughly enjoyed a career of designing for the stage that I recognize, now in hindsight, has been a winding path of chance meetings, fortuitous opportunities, and wise mentors who pointed the way for me. I have spent twenty-five years and counting designing sets for Tony award-winning directors, writers, and theatre companies across the U.S., plied those skills into designing a museum exhibit for the film *Avatar*, and continued to explore artistic collaborations in film and theme-park work. With few exceptions, each design experience was a beautiful gift not just for the resulting production that came out of the collaboration, but also for the bonds each experience forged with other artists of so many varieties: musicians, actors, writers, designers, composers, etc. Not unlike a theatrical story told onstage, my offstage story of being a designer has been full of twists, turns, and important lessons lifted from hundreds of productions with thousands of people over the years who made me a better designer because of those interactions. In a beautiful way, I have enjoyed a "front row seat" to the dedication and creativity each of those artists exhibited in each endeavor. This is a book as much about them and my observations *of* them and their creative process as it is about designing in this glorious team art form we call "theatre".

In a book she wrote called *The Creative Habit*, the great choreographer and collaborator Twyla Tharp identifies that we all possess a simple photo that may be lost to the passage of time but exists in our proverbial "mind's eye" nonetheless; one which can simply be identified as a "Mine Your Past" photo.[1] We have many photos from our childhoods, but a "Mine Your Past" photo is one that has a special place in the annals of our own personal history. It is one that does not merely show who we were at childhood age X, but *represents* the person we want to become, the dreamer we want to be, and perhaps even the adult role we would like to occupy in the world. Only in hindsight as an adult looking back on our childhood can we see the photo and say to ourselves "Well look at that ... that's when I became who I am now." Or "I always liked to do that ... I should find a way to work some of *that* joy back into my life. I LOVED doing that." Here is my "Mine Your Past" photo (see plate 1).

The year is about 1977 or so and I am "performing" a puppet show for my parents using a TV I made from a cardboard box and, as you can see, winking one eye while doing it so (of course) you can't see ME. Like virtually any child, I possessed a creative confidence and courage that we all gradually (and sadly) lose as we "mature" into adulthood. Here I am doing a puppet show on a living-room table with an audience of maybe three or four, but I am *loving* it.

I mention and articulate these memories in my preamble to "Who am I?" because I sincerely believe that it is who ALL of us are. We all have these brief moments in our memories when we can recall ourselves as our *genuinely* most creative selves. We can recall when we had that courage and abandon in our creative work and were sincerely PROUD to share it with our loved ones.

Remember that?
Remember the enthusiasm?
Remember the euphoria?
Remember the pride?

And most creative does not need to mean most *artistic*. We simply imagined ourselves to be the creators or our own worlds and shaped that world in our own way. Some of us are lucky enough to carry forward a bit of that created and creative world into our adult lives. But for those of us who did AND for those of us who did not—this book is for you. This book is for young designers when we identify ourselves as designers of our own creative fate. This book is for those willing enough—for at least a couple of hundred pages—to *imagine* ourselves as designers. This book is for those who are willing to accept the word "design" as an all-encompassing and legitimately powerful tool wielded by everyone and anyone young and old whether or not you identify yourself as "creative." Design can be both a change agent and a vehicle for that change.

> Design lets you rehearse the future.
>
> Brian Collins[2]

The Creative Adult is the Child who Survived

Approach this book like a CHILD . . . *please*?

For just this moment with this text, I ask that you submit a resignation for your current position as an adult. Give up the assumptions you know to be true as an adult and try to remember the imagination you effortlessly wielded as a child. That tree house was just as special, if not more so, than an *actual* house. The bicycle did feel like it was flying at 100 miles an hour when *you* were pedaling it. Think back and remember.

In class, I sometimes give students a minute to draw the person next to them. They frantically sketch their likeness as best they can, scribbling in and embellishing a basic stick figure perhaps or starting with an oval head and attempting to fill in the details from there. Once the "pencils down" call is made, students then laugh at themselves and at each other. What inevitably follows are a series of apologies when sharing their artwork with the neighbor next to them who was once—and perhaps never again—the subject of the artistic exercise. I hear a lot of "I'm really sorry" from the assembled class. The next comment I make, however, is meant to undermine that silliness with a (hopefully) profound observation:

Had the class been a group of eighty third graders, the apology response would be much different. And the students know it. Instead of apologies, we would most likely hear exclamations from those young kids touting their artistic masterpieces and shouting to the rooftops that these artworks must and indeed deserve to be proudly mounted on the refrigerator: the gallery of all galleries for a third grader. The Louvre for every home and a place where exceptional works of art by the smallest of family members are displayed alongside the grocery list and magnet advertising.

Kids of that age are MOST proud of their artworks. Because they don't know what they don't know, they are immensely courageous. *Imagine* if we lived our lives like that! Imagine how our world might be different if every hidden idea or artistic work in every mind on the planet had an opportunity to "come out and play" the way children play. Imagine if every crazy idea and silly notion had the courage behind it to display itself on the outside of our bodies rather than fearing a consequence each and every time we had an idea, creative thought, etc. Would those manifest themselves and sincerely make a difference in the form of a painting, a script, a poem, or an invention or an . . . anything. IMAGINE if we did not allow our fears of being vulnerable squelch each and every one of those trillions of ideas. Imagine if they did not remain hidden or unimagined in reality—what would the world look like? What might we collectively experience from a world that was a laboratory of dormant ideas, artworks, and innovations?

Einstein wrote to a colleague once: "We never cease to stand like curious **children** before the great mystery into which we are born."[3] So, I encourage you to read this book with the eyes of a child and approach the ideas proposed as malleable in your own mind in the same way an artist crafts with clay. I encourage you to not just think to yourself "Oh ... that's interesting," but also "How is this applicable to what I want to do in life?" My syllabi for many of my courses has at the top "Syllabus and Contract." The notion I impart to my design students and to you as well is that that course (and this book) is a contract. My job in the exchange is to hopefully relate some concepts and ideas related to, in this case, the art of scenic design. The reciprocal obligation on your part is to consider those concepts and ideas in the context of your own discipline, pursuit, or profession. For it is my firm belief that these concepts truly ARE applicable across boundaries because, if for no other reason, the boundaries are inherently *artificial.*

Creativity Scars

Artistic talent is something every one of us is born with in the same way we are born with parts of our bodies and toes on our feet. Every one of us is born with the ability to sleep and to dream, to show empathy for our fellow human beings, and to love and hate. As human beings, we are uniquely gifted—in the literal sense that this is *actually* a gift—to conceive of things that are not here yet. We are ALL designers. The trick is to remain a designer as we grow up.

Renowned choreographer, and author of books on creativity and collaboration, Twyla Tharp, has a theory that we all possess a creativity "scar."[4] The scar is the result of perhaps a few and perhaps many series of cuts we experience and endure throughout our lives that combine to create and convince us that we are not creative. In our very own minds, we have a belief that we certainly do NOT have talent and we certainly are NOT artistic in any way. We have all had them.

Remember that time in third grade when the teacher asked you to draw an elephant, you did, and your friend sitting next to you giggled and said "That doesn't look like an elephant at all! Looks more like a (fill in the blank) horse, turtle, name one." That's a cut! That hurt. Your feelings were hurt. You began to categorize yourself and your talent (if you even used that word) into a place in society where the majority of people reside: the "I Can't Draw So Therefore I'm Not Talented" group. Another cut follows in fourth grade and fifth grade until you pretty much not only feel, but BELIEVE that you are not talented, you do not possess any measure of creativity, and that any attempt to be creative would put you into a situation we now call an Imposter Syndrome. In the words of Sir Ken Robinson: "Instead of educating students into creativity, we instead educate them *out* of it."[5]

I ask that you be a child again with that creative confidence and courage instilled back into your bones. For the moment, you have not yet encountered any of the creativity scars that you hide now in your adult lives. You have not had the experience whereby you drew an elephant in third grade and a classmate laughed and told you it looked like a horse. You have not had any of those experiences yet. Your creative self is unblemished, and your creative soul is pure. This is an important first exercise. BE that individual again as you read this book and see the parallels between your own craft and my own in a way that hopefully allows you to feel more empowered and creative in your own field and discipline. These lessons transcend disciplines, and my hope is that illustrations and chapter entries on the design process for theatre are read with an important lesson in mind: *that you are creative*. And that creativity gives you power others have lost.

"We are all born artists." The challenge, as Picasso said, is "to remain an artist as we grow up."[6] We are all playing with materials and attempting to figure out new ways to employ it in the artform or project of our choice. Take mixing bowls, for example. We know what they ARE and what they are and should be FOR, but what else can I do with it? (See plate 2.)

Children are masters at this profound and carefree willingness to experiment with materials, to try new things, and to explore the limits of their worlds. When our own world does not suffice, children make up new ones! I spent an equal amount of time creating worlds so that I could manipulate them, create relationships, and pretend. I distinctly remember a dirt pile in the backyard that I crafted and carved into tiny trails and roads into so I could construct a miniature world using matchbox cars that "drove" all over this tiny community visiting tiny neighbors and collaborating on projects. That world served as a miniature world of my own—that I and I alone controlled—to manifest interactions between the characters I created.

An example: I designed several shows in which I wanted the effect (but not the literal use) of Spanish Moss hanging from above. As sometimes

Figure 1.1 Research Image for design of *Twelfth Night* "Amanda & The Spanish Moss". *Source: Eddie O'Bryan (photographer).*

happens, I am contracted to design shows that take place within a certain geographical boundary. For shows set in the American South, a sense of the mystery and romantic quality of Spanish Moss hanging from surrounding trees can lend just the right feel. Compare the research image for a production of *Twelfth Night* set in a turn-of-the-century Mardi Gras environment and the finished product (see plate 3).

The process of selecting a material that would be our onstage stand-in for Spanish Moss began with experimentation. "What if we use some kind of fabric strips?" which led to "What fabric already comes in strips?" which led to a discussion with a costume crafts designer who frequently makes hats to recommend something called twill tape used in making hats. Miles of twill tape dyed and dipped in paint to add some color (and some curl) and you have theatrical Spanish Moss. With an eye towards playing with the material in the same way that a child might play with aluminum foil, we can begin to see new uses and new innovations for the same (thankfully inexpensive) material. In this instance, I know what twill tape IS and I know what it is supposed to be, but what else can I do with it . . . and will it work in this marvelous magical volume we call a stage?

The point is the experimentation of the process. Artists and designers tend to think. . .with their hands.

> It's easier to act your way into a new way of thinking, than think your way into a new way of acting.
>
> Richard Pascale[7]

I hope every reader of this book will approach and digest it with the courage in your creative convictions that you had as a child. Read it with the eyes and imagination of a child and you will naturally see yourself as a designer with those same eyes. I promise.

For myself, and many of you reading this text, the next chapter beyond the puppet shows and manufactured matchbox-car worlds was high school. In my first technical theatre class, the teacher, Rick Bentley, went on to apologize that we would never "see a show the same way again." With puzzled looks, we nodded, but did not fully understand what he meant until we had some experience in the craft. Never an extrovert by any means, I became addicted to the simple idea that I could collaborate on a collective art form and never be seen! What luck! I tried virtually every aspect of technical theatre in those four years, and I relished opportunities to work as a team backstage. The choreography involved in flying scenic elements on cue and in time with music, the careful crafting of sound and lighting cues (hopefully) executed on time and in relation to the mood onstage, and the euphoria and energy involved in finishing a show with a team of likeminded dreamers was intoxicating! We felt ourselves the unsung heroes of every production. Accolades for our classmates in acting and dance were also silent accolades for us . . . a rag-tag group of nerds who did not fit in on the football team and certainly were not meant for the stage. Backstage, a sign over the stage managers podium read: "No one knows what we do until we don't do it."

Take the Risk of not Knowing

For everyone in the room, the theatre is a cathedral of ideas and experiences. It is a church for people who want to be affected by those who want to do the affecting! In this church there are no religions and no denominations. There are no ceremonial altars and candles lit in deference to a higher power. Like the theatre artists who make the theatre art, audiences arrive in a theatre giving themselves up to the story they are about to hear by fellow human beings talented enough to tell it to them—and TRANSPORT them—and affect them. It may end in laughter or tears or anger or disbelief, but theatregoers are a resilient bunch. They enjoy group catharsis. They seek the profound experience that the live theatre provides. And they look to the courageous souls of the theatre and other mediums to craft that experience for them.

Theatre artists who have experienced this euphoria know what I mean and have lived the reference. The theatre is a collective artform and one that is not for an antisocial animal. However, it CAN be for those who find joy in creating something—*anything*—together. It may be a toaster or a TV, a dance or a drama, an experience or a university. The collective whole in these situations and systems is ALWAYS greater than the sum of its parts. To this very day, I get the same joy out of a successful theatrical experience with my fellow friends and artists as I do in seeing a student I have seen grow for four full years graduate from college and take their next steps towards changing the world for the better. That "production" has, I believe, more similarities than differences. The result is different, but the euphoria remains the same. Look at what we did, what we made, what we crafted ... together!

Saying that you are a designer does not mean you are a fraud if you associate the word "designer" with only "people who can draw" or "people who are more (blank—artistic, creative, etc.)." Being a designer means, for this text at least, that you SEE the world the way a designer does. You are aware that design can be a tool for good, for change; if necessary, for revolution. To be a designer means that you are simply interested in a world that sees design as a tool for better equity and greater sustainability. Perhaps it means 3D-printing personal protective equipment for healthcare workers or a DIY ventilator for COVID patients. The point is that the moniker may seem strange and the title a little ill-fitting to you, but you are. We ALL are! To have an interest in design means you understand that there is a power in design to make visual that which we cannot otherwise comprehend. The cemetery at Arlington shows us the massive losses of multiple wars in a way that a number cannot. The world is indeed nuanced and ambiguous. Solving societal, global, and cultural challenges that result from larger populations on a smaller planet means adding a designer hat to your collection. It means that you see challenges as opportunities and constraints as a catalyst for creativity. So, dub yourself a designer at this moment with that understanding. With that title comes responsibility and awesome power. Use it for good.

As evident in this elegant quote from Robert Edmond Jones, an artist wears many hats and performs many roles:

> For the soul is a pilgrim. If we follow it, it will lead us away from our home and into another world, a dangerous world. We shall join a band of poets and dreamers, the visionaries of the theatre: the mummers, the mountebanks, the jongleurs, the minstrels, the troubadours.
>
> Robert Edmond Jones[8]

In my view, there exists a preponderance of this duality in the life of any designer or artist. You understand and embody some qualities that make you both:

- a sorcerer and an apprentice
- a believer in magic and a realist of limitations
- a dreamer and a tactician
- a cheerleader and a fan
- a leader and a follower.

There are things you *can* do and things that you *were made* to do

The theatre for the theatre artist is a cathedral of sorts. A space meant to serve as both the vessel and the means by which we collectively attempt to change minds, affect hearts, and generally ply a craft that asks an audience member to do things we wouldn't ask them to do in the "real world": suspend their disbelief so magic can happen. We craft a place where battles are fought on a nightly basis and characters rise from the floor in a pool of smoke and fog. We ask our audience to believe the Grinch can fly and that spirits are speaking to Saint Joan after she was burned at the stake. We ask our audience to essentially inhabit a space for a short time and give us the responsibility of taking them on a journey for a couple of hours. It is a theme park ride for the *soul* not the body. And every theatre artist knows that creating and holding an audience in that world is more serious than simply make believe. It is a great and profound responsibility to preserve that mystical and magical manufactured reality for as long as is needed to transport our audience somewhere for an opportunity to deeply affect them.

Think about it for a moment: Audience Member A bought a ticket and entered a sacred theatrical volume of space to see what YOU collectively came up with in your interpretation of *Hamlet* or *Seussical* or whatever piece of theatrical work you created together with your friends and collaborators. They do not exactly know what they are in for that evening. They may have a cursory idea of what they will witness, but HOW you share the story with them is completely unknown to them save the review from a friend perhaps. They take a RISK on the entire experience: the cost, the travel, and the time, yes, but perhaps more importantly, *the risk of not knowing*. They do not know what they will experience, but it will BE an experience. They *expect* to be moved. They *expect* to be taken on a journey where their assumptions are challenged, their theories are questioned, and their emotions are manipulated. They pursue what they don't know and relish in what is unpredictable. What an awesome responsibility for the theatre artist!

> The poem
> The song
> The picture
> Is only water drawn from the well
> Of the people
> And it should be given back to them
> In a cup of beauty
> So that they may drink
> And in drinking
> Understand themselves
>
> Federico García Lorca[9]

Back to you: the young designer. How can you affect change? Perhaps a more relevant question is how can you *not* affect change? I follow a guru of higher education on Twitter by the name of Bryan Alexander. He is an author and hosts a weekly video podcast called the Future Trends Forum whereby he assembles educators in a virtual room to discuss pressing topics of the day, share data on trends in higher ed, and generally defers to his audience and what they want to discuss. In that context and by his own admission, he refers to himself as "chief cat herder." The man is also a futurist. A testimonial on his website proclaims, "Many calls themselves 'futurists'—Bryan actually knows how to do it."[10] And based on a definition of futurist (a person who studies the future and makes predictions about it based on current trends) he is also arguably very good at it. He analyzes data, makes estimates of potential trajectories, surmises multiple pathways that data could take us, and makes educated guesses on what is on the horizon for higher education. We must put futurist thinking into practice not just our artform but for every aspect of our society.

> We in the theatre ... our job is to try to hold up a vision to America that shows not only who all of us are individually, but that welds us back into the

> commonality that we need to be, the sense of unity, the sense of whole, the sense of who we *are as a country*. That's what the theatre is supposed to do, and that's what we need to try to do as well as we can.
>
> Oskar Eustis[11]

Now think for a moment about what you—as a designer—do. You discuss a written piece of work in a collaborative team, analyze it, explore the themes, adapt it as needed, and eventually offer up multiple (we hope) scenarios for spaces in which that story can be told. One version might be more formal, another upside down and backwards. One may be a sandbox in complete disarray, another may be meticulously curated to a great degree. What does the play "say"? A designer is asked to interpret that language with others and create a volume that speaks at least part of that story to an audience when they enter a room. I would argue that designers are inherent futurists. They combine the possible with the plausible to come up with the probable. That is our role now.

You are a Designer Everyday

You awoke this morning and presumably got dressed. You began in a way that dreams up what you are going to be doing that day: are you riding a bike or meeting with an important client. You take stock of what you will be doing and, from that, how you need to look in order to make an impression (or not) on the people you'll come in contact with that day. You reviewed and empathized with your future self a bit later in the day, made an assessment in your mind of what you need to wear to pull off the important meeting or ride 5 miles on your bike . . . and made clothing decisions from there. THAT was a creative act!

From there, you had an idea of what you want to wear. Not a fully fleshed-out down to the cuff-links idea, but an idea. You think to yourself: "Today would be a good day to wear that gray blazer with that blue shirt and maybe the jeans with it since I've got a more casual day ahead of me." You have an idea. That is your second creative act of the morning.

You paired those shoes with those pants and that shirt. You matched the blouse and skirt in a way to you, looking the mirror at yourself, looked like a good combination—of color, of grayscale value, of formality or informality. You prototyped the look THAT was your third creative act and in a span of the first fifteen minutes of your day no less.

You may reevaluate and essentially test your attire later in the day for practicality and utility. Perhaps you underestimated the humidity and really should have gone with the linen over the corduroy. Perhaps the jeans were a bad choice because you had that one meeting with an important client that was tacked on to your day last minute. What you are doing is testing your idea out: logging information for the next time you get dressed.

Your attire was a five-step process of evaluating, defining, ideating, prototyping, and testing. If my earlier reference did not convince you to wear the moniker—and wear it proudly—this should: that process makes you a designer. We are ALL designers of different specialties, levels, and experiences. What you completed in the "getting dressed" exercise was a 5-step process of Design Thinking.

Pioneered by a company called IDEO in Palo Alto, California co-founded by Dave and Tom Kelley, Design Thinking has gradually elevated the role of a designer in today's world to a level never seen before in the profession. The idea behind it is simple: design and design thinking can be a tool and a process to iterate new solutions to old and new problems. The key is a collaborative team-oriented mindset centered around building on the ideas of others in a group. Groups are comprised of individuals from a diverse set of backgrounds so varying perspectives are looking at the same challenge. A group could be comprised of a musician, a psychologist, an engineer, an anthropologist, and a physicist . . . and that would be just fine. Actually, it would be *ideal*!

What should become readily apparent to anyone that has served on a creative team for a theatrical production are the similarities with the design thinking process outlined above and the theatrical design process. You have

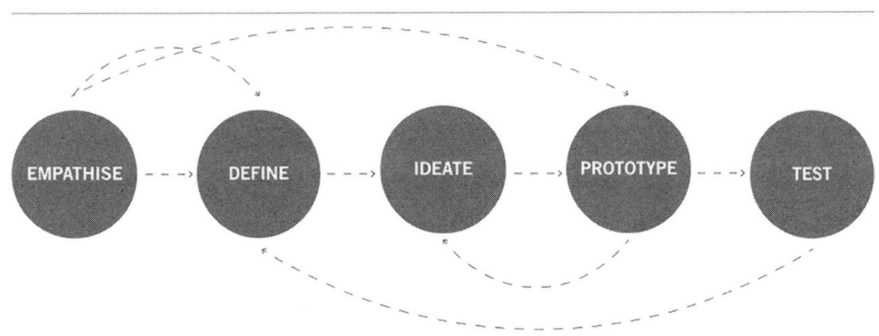

Figure 1.2 The Five Phases of the Design Thinking Process. *Source: Jean-Patrice Rémillard with pheek.com.*

been doing this all along. You got this. This process is second nature to you and the possibilities of how, if you wish, you might apply it outside of the realm of theatre design are practically limitless. Inherent in you as a theatre person are these qualities. You naturally build on the remarkable diversity of skills, experiences, and backgrounds in virtually every creative team and rely on the fact that all involved (at least presumably) want to make something . . . *together*.

Something that is well known among educators is the *Last Lecture* by Randy Pausch. Afflicted with a cancer and with little time left to live, Professor Randy Pausch at Carnegie Mellon delivered what has become known as the "last lecture." In it, he describes what he calls a "head fake" method of teaching otherwise known as indirect learning.[12] The method is essentially a way to trick a student into learning. While a student is having fun, collaborating with classmates, or completing an exercise they indirectly learn a profound concept. You just experienced this head fake concept in reading the process of your typical morning getting dressed and evaluating your work at that particular task. Hopefully, you not only see yourself as creative (the head fake), but you should also see yourself as a *designer*! And we have the design thinking process to prove it. You do it every day, but perhaps had not thought of it as design.

Building on that diversity of skills and experiences is key, but so is being comfortable with ambiguity and uncertainty. As a design teacher of mine used to say, "at some point, you have to quit aiming and fire." Designers of all kinds need to embrace the simple truth that sometimes you must act without all the information, and you have to jump without any certainty whatsoever that there will be a net to catch you. Designers need to see themselves and the world with "designer eyes": understanding that BOTH are a work in progress. Neither is perfect and, arguably, neither will ever be truly completed. Ambiguity and uncertainty surround us. Live with it and not against it.

Ansel Adams and Georgia O'Keefe: Both colleagues and artists had a fascination of the American West in the early part of the twentieth century. The content for those Western environments served as inspiration for their artworks throughout their career. But that's where similarities between the two art icons *ends*. Georgia O'Keefe took a close-up and sensual approach to her work rife with brilliant colors and Ansel Adams carefully curated black-and-white images of landscapes taken from a distance to the point that finer details typical of Georgia's work are lost in deference to an almost spiritual perspective in Ansel's work. To take them in together means flipping the switch on your perspective from extreme close-up and an almost-magnified view (Georgia's work) to a colorless and much more distant take on the same environment (Ansel's work). Design also requires a designer to flip back and forth between perspectives as often as possible. To look at something with fresh eyes and, perhaps more importantly, a fresh mind can make all the difference when judging your own designs and making choices about your next move, or change, or revision to it. The hope is to draw comparisons into view in a way that allows you, the reader, to see consider your artform as a young designer to be applicable across a spectrum of opportunities and professions. The result will be a transformation of the way you see yourself, your opportunities, and your perspectives when viewing this new world of design with "designer eyes".

Like an O'Keefe painting, stage design is a world where realistic volumes in which we live our day-to-day need not exist. A kitchen and a living room may be described, but we designers work in a wonderland of possibility where the rules need not apply to this special volume—this wondrous space—this sacred air. Once we realize that a designed volume onstage need not "follow the rules" of engagement of the rest of our lives outside of that volume, we are truly LIBERATED. We can proceed with embracing the work with a childlike sensibility full of wonder and curiosity. We can proceed knowing that things like flying carpets, invisible men, and "air vibrations" (stay with me) are indeed possible. It's the magic that drew us into the craft and creating more magic is why we stick with it after all.

Take this story from an assistant for the great designer Franco Zeffirelli describing the model building process of a 1972 design for *Don Giovanni*:

> His visual ideal was an exquisitely pretty and charming set in Watteau colors, suffused with all the technical magic the opera house could provide. On a steep and foreshortened slope that ended ... into the sky, scenic elements sliding on rails or flown in from the grid appeared as if by magic to fuse into an ever-changing tableau. The resulting scenes with their kinetic impact enhanced by exquisite lighting were intended to give the effect of engravings; their characteristic horizontal striations were to convey the impression of "air vibrations".
>
> It is easy to reproduce these strokes on a piece of paper, but to do so in three-dimensions is quite a different matter. This problem preoccupied Zeffirelli a great deal, and at first it was difficult to see how the theory could be put into practice.
>
> One day we were sitting at his studio in Rome, discussing the problem and illustrating our points with sketches. When it seemed to me that there was no

practical solution to our predicament, Zeffirelli walked out of the room. Soon afterwards he reappeared, beaming with delight; he held a packet of spaghetti in his hand.

For a moment, I was unsure whether or not this was an invitation to a traditional lunch. Then all became clear. "I've got it," he exclaimed. He spread some glue on a sheet of glass and stuck pieces of spaghetti horizontally across it to produce what looked like a three-dimensional flat.

The construction of these backcloths . . . proved much more difficult than sticking spaghetti to glass. We had to cut up some 17,000 metros of PVC conduit into twenty-mere tubes and thread them on thin wires at intervals of one to two centimetres, the final result resembling a gigantic blind. Next, these "air vibrators" were painted and Zeffirelli was right; the effect of these unorthodox contrivances on the stage was sensational.

I confine myself to this one example, because it was so typical: the spaghetti idea could not have come to Zeffirelli out of the blue, he simply chose it as a visual demonstration of a solution that had been maturing in his mind. Banal things like this best demonstrate an artist's relationship to his material, and his talent for clarifying complex ideas using simple means.

My work with Zeffirelli proved a lasting theatrical experience and confirmed my view that the great masters are simple men at heart.[13]

Two Worlds that Collide at the Stage Edge

It has only been recently that I have been struck with the purpose of the theatre—and its differences from other artistic mediums. What drives theatre artists to do what they do for hours and weeks at a time in a dark theatre with little to no access to natural light in a medium that asks so much of all its participants—from long hours to strained relationships and wallets? What IS it that keeps theatre artists coming back again-and-again to struggle to represent someone onstage who is not themselves and strive to create just the right mood and stage picture to evoke a feeling in an audience member whether that is achieved by light or color or costume? Why? Why keep trying? Why keep rehearsing to "get it right . . ." whatever that means? The profession asks so much of its servants. And yet. The march towards creating new work and new worlds onstage continues anew each year in countless theatres large and small across the globe in so many forms and with so much on the line in terms of personal and financial cost to the performers and artists attempting (and not always succeeding) to draw a line at the stage edge and craft a false reality upstage of it.

Perhaps it is about that very line of magic at the stage edge. What I mean is that, like the matchbox car dirt pile community, what we collectively craft upstage of the line at the stage is an alternate reality. The story of that reality is the script, and the evocation of that reality is on the shoulders of the entire production and creative team upstage of that edge. Sometimes the world is fantastical and at times naturalistic. Sometimes beautiful and sometimes terrifying or ugly. But regardless of what it IS, what we DO upstage of it is entirely up to the collaboration of the artists who inhabit this pretend world onstage. What an incredible power to create—without a movie screen—a world that, for an audience is perhaps foreign to their own or perhaps very familiar. We jest about "smoke and mirrors" to deceive an audience, but the stage world can be a mirror that reflects back to an audience a different perspective and a different reality. For two hours, we craft a world that supports an ideal or depicts a moment in time that is occupied by artists in costume who are masters at getting us to truly believe that their world actually exists—if only for two hours—and we are voyeurs into it. What a marvelous crucible of space! What an amazing experience for a show to be a theme-park ride for the soul. For those audience members willing to suspend their disbelief, an entire journey begins at the rise (or not) of the curtain thus beginning an emotional journey to the end.

But what of that proverbial "line"? Should we agree that the line exists at all, is it fluid? In other words, what happens when the line shifts into the audience to include them—at least emotionally—into the story being told onstage. For a while, we as an audience member, exist in parallel worlds and perhaps parallel time periods. When done right and when we truly *believe*, the world onstage becomes ours as well as the world offstage where our families and our cars and our homes are. We straddle that line for a while and entice it to make us feel something or understand something or be someone else for a moment in time. The story onstage is an *exchange* and a reality and false reality become fluid.

I am reminded of a production of the *Diary of Anne Frank* that I designed adapted by Wendy Kesselman whereby we chose to encircle the audience quite literally with barbed wire as they entered the space and march SS officers around the perimeter of the theatrical volume during portions of the show. An SS marching song and actual costumed Nazi officers marched around, for example, just prior to Anne awakening her roommate Mr. Dussel from a nightmare she was experiencing. The experience was collectively designed by multiple artists to generate a visceral feeling on the part of the audience of being IN the annex with the occupants. I would argue that, at that moment, the "line" of reality shifted to include them and encourage them to experience the world in a way and in a style that was deeply emotional and visceral. The end of the same show included a soundscape brilliantly designed by Jane Shaw to include the deep rumbling and passing of a train over the entire audience only to end in a shrill and sudden screech of noise of the train leaving our world and entering what—at that time—was a dark and mysterious hellscape for children like Anna. A deep black void from which no one returned. The only actual surviving member of the Annex, Otto Frank, descends into the space past the audience, crosses to the middle of the stage, turns 180 degrees, gently removes his hat, and begins a monologue to the audience that deeply and profoundly affects every person in the room:

MR. FRANK (Directly to us.)
Westerbork. A barren heath. Wooden towers where our jailers stand guard. Walls covered with thousands of flies. The eight of us crammed into Barrack 67—betrayed. We never know by whom. Our last month together.

(He pauses.)

Our last month. Anne and Peter walking hand in hand between the barracks and barbed wire. Edith worrying about the children, washing underclothing in murky water, numb. Margot, silent, staring at nothing. Our last days on Dutch soil.

(Pause.)

Late August, Paris freed. Brussels, Antwerp. But for us it is too late. Tuesday September third, 1944, a thousand of us herded into cattle cars, the last transport to leave Westerbork for the extermination camps.

The train. Three days, three nights. In the middle of the third night . . . Auschwitz. Separation. Men from women. Edith. Margot. Anne. My family. Never again. Selection. Half our transport killed in the gas chambers. One day Peter and I see a group of men march away, his father among them. Gassed. Peter on the "death march" to Mauthausen. Dead three days before the British arrive. His mother—Auschwitz, Bergen-Belsen, Buchenwald, Theresienstadt—date of death unknown. Mr. Dussel dies in Neuengamme.

(Pause.)

January twenty-seventh, 1945. I am freed from Auschwitz. I know nothing of Edith and the children. And then I learn . . . Edith died in Birkenau of grief, hunger, exhaustion.

(Pause.)

The winter of '45, typhus breaks out in Bergen-Belsen, killing thousands of prisoners, among them Margot. Anne's friend, Hanneli, sees Anne through the barbed wire, naked, her head shaved, covered with lice. "I don't have anyone anymore," she weeps. A few days later, Anne dies. My daughters' bodies dumped into mass graves, just before the camp is liberated.

(MR. FRANK bends down, picks up ANNE's diary lying on the floor. He steps forward, the diary in his hands.)

All that remains.[14]

Following a preview performance of the production, we designers and members of the creative team typically stay in the theatre for production notes from the director. In essence, we occupy this magical crucible of space long after the houselights come up and the audience departs. We are well into our work and discussion of what went well and what went wrong by the time audience members have arrived at their homes and are (hopefully) talking about what they witnessed and how they felt.

On one particular preview night, after one specific preview performance, I was struck by a simple display a few rows in front of me: a woman stood by her husband's side holding his hand. He was still seated and appeared to be having trouble moving at all. His head was down. His wife holding his hand in an almost dutiful way awaiting him to recover and supporting him in his attempt to get to that place. He briefly removed his baseball cap long enough for me to see that he was wearing a yarmulke underneath. What I felt come over me perhaps *should* have been sadness or empathy for his situation. For what the "collective we" **did** to him. What this production, this experience, this story **did** to him. I am a bit ashamed to say that I instead felt pride for my small part in affecting this one individual in such a profound way as to cause him to have difficulty even *moving* after having experienced it.

Ever since, I have been struck by the question of what exactly *happened* there? What did we—or he—do to have that depth of an experience with a theatre production and, if we want to, how do we do that AGAIN? How do we affect an audience and perhaps even change their mind about something in as close to a lived experience as we can make it? How do we generate a group catharsis? In this case, we succeeded in transporting an individual to a different time and place buoyed by a moving story in a way that affected him not only emotionally but also physically. In an odd way, for any theatre artist, that is a WIN. How do we get back to that? How do we recreate that for not only one person, but multiple people? Doing so is not easy and having a production "fire on all cylinders" can be more rare than common almost certainly. But that does not keep us from trying—again and again.

The theatre muse is elusive and that is why we chase it. That is why we spend hours attempting to craft a series of moments and a volume of magic to help a perhaps-unwilling audience to GO on the journey and give up themselves and their reality for just a little while ... just long enough to (when it works) affect them in a way that may manifest itself into the inability to move after it is over. The theatre is our church, and our faith is in the power of the story we are telling an audience of our peers. What a marvelous reality to craft and what a significant *responsibility* we have in our attempts to achieve that false reality.

When the "line" shifts to include an audience, magical things happen. We are transported. We are affected. We are forever changed.

2

Empathy and Answering, "What Story Are We Telling?" with Collaborators

Chapter Outline

The Beginning of the Design Journey—and the Possibility Represented by "What If? . . ."

The late Sir Ken Robinson once articulated the "powers" that you and I possess that are uniquely human in a speech on "Imagination and Empathy":

> "What identifies us as human beings above all are the powers that flow from our deep resource of imagination . . . we have evolved this powerful sense of imagination at least to bring to mind things that aren't here. And from it flow all kinds of powers like creativity and, uniquely and distinctly, the power of

> empathy: the ability to put yourself in someone else's position and imagine might that might be like."
>
> Sir Ken Robinson[1]

It is in this spirit that all humans must consider what we actually *do* with these powers in imagining things that are not there. In the theatre world, that is essentially what we do in creative teams for about 90 percent of the production process: imagine things that are not there … yet. The first meeting of a creative team around a table discussing the "world of the play" represents a fleeting moment of endless possibility—an empathetic phase that drives a good (or bad) process moving forward. We enter a world where there exists enormous possibility *and* opportunity in tossing around ideas and words, dreams and visions, and impressions about the written work. This can be one of the most exciting moments of the entire design process for a play (or musical or movie or . . .). It is a moment when all the "what if's" and "whys" and "what's" are on the proverbial table.

- Why are we doing this play at this time in this period in history?
- Why are we telling this story?
- Why do we feel an obligation to present this piece now?
- What statement are we making to our audience?
- What do we hope to "reflect back" to them?
- What do we want the audience to be discussing on the car ride home after they see it?
- What would make a production of this play suck? (A great question honestly!)
- What if we rise Prospero up from below on an enormous lift in a gown covered in mirrors?
- What if Dracula was seen in a coffin with red eyes that scan the audience to end the Act?
- What if the prince disappeared in smoke and a strobe effect that blinded the audience?

Key to this opportunity at interaction is a simple yet difficult to achieve core understanding among collaborators: that we are *collaborating*! The word may be a cliché now, but we have entered a "safe-space" as collaborators. As important as the ideas shared is the spirit in which they are shared. It is crucial to create a secure creative environment where crazy ideas and stupid questions can be asked. As an example, two equally important questions may be asked in this phase that underscore the lesson here:

1 Why must we assume that Hamlet *see* his dead father in order to believe the message?
2 Why are we assuming that the core message of the experience we offer our customers is X when it could be X + Y? . . . or just Y . . . or just Z?

In the true spirit of the "why," we should step back a bit and ask ourselves: What makes crazy ideas and stupid questions so important to the creative process anyway? How are those useful? Why should we prioritize a spirit that invites them into our creative spaces? Great questions!

The answers all begin with empathy . . . and actors.

With empathy being a catchphrase of late to describe "the ability to understand and share the feelings of another," I contend that is indeed ACTORS who perhaps are the most empathetic souls with the most experience in empathy. Great actors convince you, the audience member, that they indeed ARE the character they are playing whether it be an historical figure or a fictional character. Consider the best performance you've ever seen: what made you truly *believe* the story had to, in large part, be credited to the ability of the actor to make you believe . . . in them.

In *The Dramatic Imagination*, Robert Edmond Jones perhaps articulates the process of acting best:

> Great roles require great natures to interpret them. Half our pleasure in seeing a play lies in our knowledge that we are in the presence of artists. But this pleasure of watching the artists themselves is soon forgotten, if the play is well performed, in the contagious excitement of watching a miracle: the miracle of incarnation. For acting is a process of incarnation. Just that. And it is a miracle. I have no words to express what I feel about this subtle, ancient, sacred art—the marvel of it, the wonder, the meaning . . . The actor creates in his (or her) living self. And just as the good designer retires in favor of the actor, so does the good actor withdraw his (or her) personal self in favor of the character they are playing.[2]

Now that's empathy! Empathy has become an important consideration in the business realm as the companies have come to realize that they truly need to understand and design for their "end-user" across all spectrums from experiences to systems to products.

And when you think of collaboration and empathy, what better instructors in that regard than theatre professionals?

One evening, Peter Amster, a dear friend and director, and myself were talking over a meal and discussing some of his methods in directing actors towards a journey where they are better equipped to "find their character."

When approached by an actor having difficulty on how to say a line, his advice was as simple as it was profound. He said "Say it like you're Johnny Cash!" Saying the line in the voice of Johnny Cash is rarely, if ever, the correct advice. Saying the lines . . .

> This above all: to thine own self be true,
> And it must follow, as the night the day,
> Thou canst not then be false to any man.[3]
>
> quote by Polonius in Shakespeare's *Hamlet*, Act I, Scene 3

. . . like you are Johnny Cash is always the *wrong* approach.

But here's the rub:

Saying that line like you are Johnny Cash is an important place to be as an actor. It is, in fact, the intentionally *wrong* place to be with that character, BUT the journey *from* the wrong reading *to* the correct one is a journey worth taking. It is a journey full of discovery about that character, about yourself, about the message the playwright has in mind, and about the responsibility of the actor to play that role in a certain way. So often we focus on the end-goal and we overlook the importance of the journey! The *journey* is where growth occurs, and creation happens.

Imagine ANY of the Tolkien novels or movies *without* the journey?
Imagine the *Star Wars* saga or any hero tale of any kind *without* the journey?
Without the journey, the *Odyssey* isn't an odyssey at all.
Without the journey, the *Godfather* series has no middle—just a beginning and an end.

Creating Creative Space

In 2009, a young playwright and composer was writing political jingles when he read a biography by a historian named Ron Chernow that reminded him of the rapper Tupac Shakur. It was via that intellectual and artistic leap in thought that the idea for the musical *Hamilton* was born. The playwright was Lin-Manuel Miranda who had to have a thick skin and an insatiable drive to pursue what would become one of the most successful musicals of all time. While it's easy to appreciate the success of a musical that grossed $600K per week in ticket sales in 2016 *today*, imagine Lin-Manuel pitching that idea to YOU before a word was written or a note played. Be honest: would you have thought he was crazy? Would you need some serious convincing to appreciate the novelty of an idea that means to tell the story of a founding father (without a father) by way of hip-hop music ... and with a cast as diverse as our country itself? The end of the story of that musical has been written, but it is the beginning of the story which can truly inspire and serve as a testament to one single creative idea mixed with resilience and determination.

It is *precisely* that type of environment that must exist for truly creative and innovative ideas to flourish.

And while it may be easy to formally "adopt" or say we intend to foster an environment that welcomes crazy ideas and stupid questions, far too often we setup our collaboration spaces—both literally and figuratively—in a way that works against that spirit of collaboration.

First, the literal space. While we may think the room where we meet is inconsequential, consider these two images side-by-side (see plate 4).

The image of the long rectangular table creates an unspoken power dynamic that nonverbally relates a notion that the person at the end of the table approves or disapproves of ideas placed before them. The image on the right shares this same perceived power equally. It may seem like a minor detail, but the arrangement of creative team members around a table—any table—really makes a difference in setting up an environment where team members feel equal and ideas are welcomed and not judged by others. When this dynamic is working and collaborative synapses are firing between members of the creative team, it may seem like virtually anything is possible! Limitations begin to feel like minor obstacles in the face of the collective creativity and uniqueness of ideas that a collaborative table can create together.

Secondly, the figurative "space." What fosters—and what doesn't—a creative space where there is freedom among ALL participants (including the introverts) to offer up crazy ideas and ask stupid questions?

One of the biggest obstacles in that endeavor? FEAR. We fear the judgement of others. Even artists do!

Fear that our artwork is not even artwork AT ALL. Fear that we don't belong in the pantheon of "more talented" or "more established" artists. We imagine instead a line of assembled judges clutching large numbers awaiting the conclusion of our skate, to publicly judge our work on a world stage. Sounds crazy, but most artists—even those that are internationally renowned—believe it.

So how do we overcome that fear? The first step is realizing the dynamics of the assembled members of the creative team. As a collective whole, we are certainly led by the theatre organization that hired us, by the director who chose us to be on that team, and by the play/musical/film/etc. that we are tasked to make visual. In that context, we must also realize that we are equal collaborators brought to the table to make something together, to dream up a world and a space that looks a certain way and sounds a certain way and feels a certain way based on what we *collectively* believe is the proper vehicle for the story being told onstage. There exists an important point here: that the first design meeting is not only an opportunity for a thoughtful speech by the director on why it is important to produce the play, or why the play was chosen to be included in the season, but it must also be a gathering of ideas and musings and pontifications of all kinds from ALL the creative team members.

The first design meeting should be a gathering of souls who have all found "a way in" to the piece we are tasked with producing. We must recognize that our individual avenues into the world of the play may be different. To use the *Hamlet* example again, two different creative team members may each find different ways to respond to the piece. One person may believe the piece is about betrayal and retribution for that betrayal and another may believe it is about a son's extreme devotion to family. BOTH are correct! BOTH deserve discussion at that first meeting.

A creative team assigned to design a production can be a revealing window into group dynamics and the need for the right figurative and literal environment. It is in these meetings that we can think of the design process as an inverted cone that young designers will traverse through the entirety of the design process.

The first design meeting exists at the top of this inverted cone where we are determining the "world of the play" including everything from the volume of space to the layering of the costumes and from the sounds of the aural architecture surrounding us to the quality of light streaming through windows and alleyways. The team is collectively asking (and perhaps answering) big questions as to the world, time period, and level of realism or abstraction that suits THIS particular production best for THIS particular audience in THIS particular city and at THIS particular time in history.

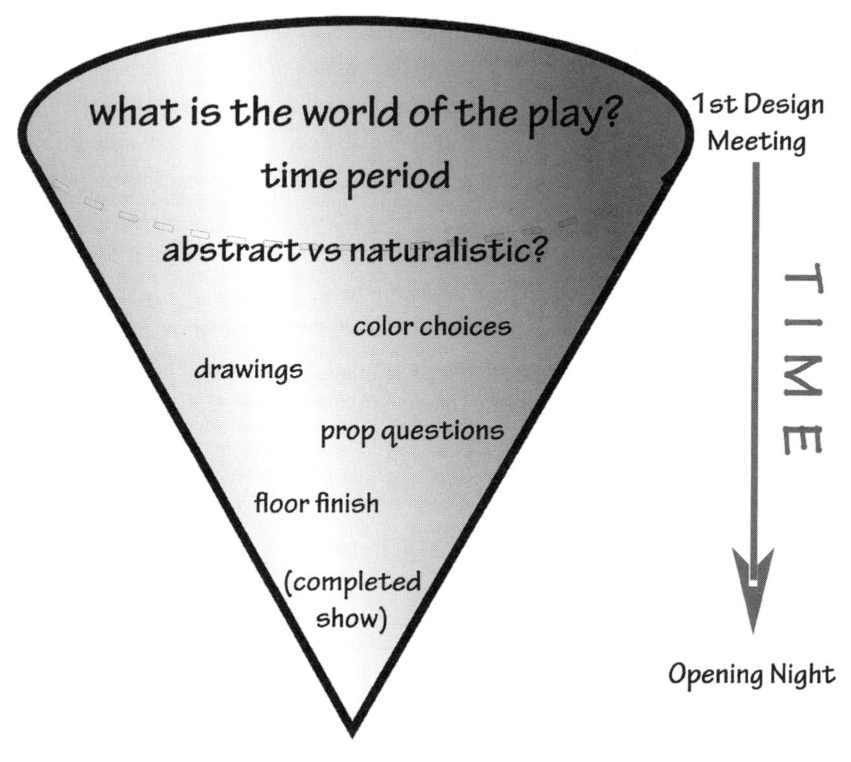

Figure 2.1 Inverted Cone Process of Design Ideas. *Source: graphic by author.*

The Design Jacket and how it Fits (or Does Not Fit) the Play

One might think of this designed world as a jacket meant to fit itself upon the piece of written work (play, film, exhibit, etc.) that we are collectively tailoring together. To use the *Hamlet* example yet again, the director and design team may answer our "what if . . ." statement with "What if we set Hamlet on the moon?" What follows (or at least should follow) should be a discussion about whether Hamlet-on-the-Moon (a sequel to *Einstein on the Beach*?) is a story worth being told for your audience and do the themes translate. Do we tweak the Marcellus' line in Act I, Scene 4: "Something is rotten in the state of Denmark" to "Something is rotten in the Copernicus crater"?[4] And what does that even mean? Does it translate? The design-jacket may not fit.

But let's find a better "jacket" example, shall we?

Richard III is a play written by Shakespeare around 1593 and depicts the rise to power of Richard III of England by means of murder and deception following the re-accession to the throne of his brother, King Edward IV of England. Considered an outcast, Richard lashes out and states his intentions in just the first scene: "I am determined to prove a villain / And hate the idle pleasures of these days."[5]

For a viable conceptual "jacket", take the 1995 film, starring Ian McKellen as Richard III, with a narrative updated to the 1930s and a murderous character in Richard who adopts fascistic tendencies and aligns himself with a Nazi-esque dictatorship in order to acquire the power he seeks. By all accounts, the narrative falls into place and the updated story "works" to make it more immediate and relatable to the audience.

If/Then as a Catalyst for Design Ideas

Just as important as finding that jacket are the conversations that lead up to that discovery. How do we begin digging into a script with a level of childlike curiosity that can drive a meaningful dialogue towards a conceptual "jacket"? Why not begin with some if/then statements?

If this play were a (blank), what type of (blank) would it be?

1. Color:
2. Music:
3. Painter:
4. Book:
5. Animal:
6. Film/movie:
7. Drink:
8. Sport:
9. Celebrity:
10. Character (invent one, be descriptive—age, weight, hair, etc.)

Seems a bit ridiculous at first but answering just a few of these questions can lead to some profound opinions and approaches to almost any piece of writing. One creative team member might think the play is red, while another may see it as more of a blue play. The conversation justifying both of those answers is where deep insights about the work begins!

In my work directing a university-level interdisciplinary program, I must often answer to parents (less so to students) that the mere concept of disciplines and individualized areas of study is relatively new, dating back to the initial organizational development of higher educational institutions in the eighteenth century. The boundaries we have established between disciplines and the silos that are created as a result are essentially the intellectual shackles, we have placed on ourselves. Prior to the eighteenth century, the great thinkers of the world ignored these divisions and were intensely curious across those disciplines. Renaissance thinkers like DaVinci and Michelangelo found curious new inspirational opportunities across disciplines that spanned literature to engineering to architecture. Renowned as an artist and sculptor, Michelangelo began work on St. Peter's Basilica at age *seventy-one* after much prodding from the Pope himself. Einstein reveled in combining concepts to create new ideas and new approaches to complex problems. He marveled at the world in a way that a child might marvel at seeing snow for the first time.

> There are only two ways to live your life. One is as though nothing is a miracle.
> The other is as though everything is a miracle.
>
> Albert Einstein[6]

Renaissance Teams

Design teams can and should emulate a team of Renaissance thinkers gathered to discuss the design of an experience—or a table—or a building—or a play. There should be as many bright minds that represent a gathering of as many disciplines as possible so that we thereby cover as many areas—and therefore ideas—as possible when we are in the "What if . . ." phase and beyond.

Designer Bruce Mau has put together a list of qualifications for members of any Renaissance team:

1. *Expertise*—each person must have deep knowledge in the field they represent.
2. *Curiosity*—a Renaissance Team player WANTS to know about other things.
3. *Empathy*—they must know how to listen, be respectful of other people, and have the ability and willingness to imagine other experiences and perspectives.

4 *Confidence*—each member of the team must be willing to lead. Depending on the solution the team designs, it may make more sense for one expert to lead it into execution (i.e., the digital expert, or the data guy, or the film producer).
5 *Humility*—each member of the team must be willing to follow. Don't assume everyone has this skill.
6 Independence—each expert must have a mind and voice of their own and the ability to offer an outlier's perspective, even a critical one.
7 *Courage*—members must be willing to share imaginative, even crazy ideas and trust the team and the iterative design process.

It is important to remember that the team organized is comprised of human beings in a world increasingly dominated by automation and AI-driven technologies. At a time when assembly lines and human jobs are rapidly being replaced by machines, we need to realize our true value and our uniqueness as a human race. It is on these creative teams that a young designer should realize that our powers of empathy and human understanding are what set us apart from professions that require little human face-to-face interaction and artistic contribution. That is the collaborative engine. What makes the product of these meetings unique is entirely due to the unique voices around the collaborative table. The art we create today should reflect the world we live in today! A tired production that only means to recreate and not reflect back is one we have all seen before—and have no desire to see again.

Saying something along the lines of "I think the play is about loss" is a MUCH more interesting directive than having a team of designers ask what color the set should be or what texture the floor should have. At such an early stage in the process, that is waaay too early to be asking such questions.

A limited budget can also drive a first design meeting in the wrong direction. While the realities of limited resources may be a consideration at some point, do not let them seep into the first design discussion about the piece. I was mentoring some students producing an unsupported student production of *Dead Man's Cell Phone* some years ago and the collected voices met to discuss the production at the first design meeting. Having read the piece, but not wanting to influence the proceedings or the final outcome, I told the students that I would just be a "fly on the wall" for their meeting, only interjecting when necessary. The students briefly discussed the venue and dates for the production and then went into a laundry list of what they thought was important based on the script we all had read:

"So, scene X calls for Y number of chairs. Anyone know where we can get Y chairs?"

"Anyone have a dead cell phone they're not using anymore that we could use as a prop one?"

Unable to quiet myself any longer, I interjected: "Wait, wait. Hang on. What is this play ABOUT? Why are you doing it? HOW do we want to affect the audience that sees it? What KIND of world is best for this play? Maybe just maybe, less may be more here?"

The team agreed that we had skipped over what is arguably the most exciting period of the entire process: the "What if . . .?" phase. What if the entire space was not real (whatever that means) *at all*? What do we gain and what do we lose if the audience walks into a completely abstract volume of space? It is essential to focus on these big, broad, bold questions in the early phase of any team meeting. Get to the WHY we are doing it at all! What is the payoff? How do we want to lead into the future and what do we truly and deeply want to create together? Theatre does that for many people. It is a deeply collaborative art form that welcomes anyone of any background into the fold and essentially asks "What do WE want to say . . . TOGETHER?" What do we seek to understand? What is the voice we want to raise and the story we want to tell? THAT'S the crux of it. That is the essence. These are BIG questions that must be answered . . . *before* we figure out if we need chairs.

3

The Importance of Research as "Fuel" for ANY Process

Chapter Outline

The Playlist of the Mind

Let's ponder a thought experiment for a moment: let us consider your brain (and mine) as a playlist of experiences, influences, and inspirations in your life along the lines of the songs you have in your pocket on your phone. With that as a premise, what are your "favorites"? As you browse the files of your mind, what memories do you have of being truly inspired? How did those memories and experiences shape who you are and are there clues in those life experiences (phrases in each song) that truly resonate with you? The soundtrack of your life has all kinds of clues buried in it that deserve a closer look. I have a high-school classmate and higher-ed colleague at the

University of Texas, Dr. Michael Webber, who wrote the following about his own lived experience and how that led him to devise a course that played to those experiences:

> My memories as a student are always crisper and happier from the times we were out of the classroom. By contrast, my memories from inside the classroom were foggy at best. Using that perspective, I thought it would be fun to create a class where the classroom is purely administrative and walking around looking at things would be the place where actual learning takes place.[1]

The course took students to a cement quarry and kiln, a Walmart distribution center, a sewage treatment plant, a recycling center, a data center, a power plant, and a solar panel factory. These lived experiences are hard to forget and move the content of the classroom to lived moments in time.

To use another analogy, consider your memories as drops in a pond you create every day of your life. Some days offer few memories and perhaps the pond is nothing more than a puddle when the day is done. Other days offer many larger and more frequent droplets of memories and experiences that make that day—or that week—or that month—particularly meaningful when looking back on the rain-gauge of your life. Consider these moments in life as a "high-water mark" of sorts when inspiration and flow were easy to access, and memories of that day are fresh in your mind. What ABOUT those days stays with you? And I don't mean what *happened*? I mean what ABOUT those happenings allow you to easily remember and access that memory? Was it joy, sorrow, epiphany, or loss? As you reflect, you may even get a visceral sense of standing outside of yourself watching yourself experience that memory for the very first time. Of those memories, which ones can and should fall under the category of "inspiration." Perhaps it was a moment in class when a teacher's comment struck a chord or when you were exposed to a piece of artwork that changed your opinion or your outlook on the world. What were you doing? What did you say at that moment and perhaps only to yourself? The human creature is one who speaks aloud moments that have a deep impact on us. Did you say "wow . . . what is this?" and if so, what was THAT??

I contend that designers and aspiring designers of any flavor have an ability to access this playlist-of-the-mind and draw upon those experiences to make new experiences, or artworks, or systems. To find yourself in tune with that playlist of memories means that you can channel that into your work in a way that is allows you to form a new piece of "music" with that experienced memory as your muse. Try it for a moment. What is your most easily accessed memory from:

1 last week?
2 last month?
3 last year?

What is the first memory that pops into your mind when you think of your summer vacation, your spring break, your winter, your fall?

It is my solemn belief that THOSE experiences are the roadmap we as artists and as professionals consistently overlook when looking for both inspiration and life-design guidance. We have a notion that our work and our life are separate entities that do not necessarily need to co-exist or even agree across an (artificial) divide. How strange is that? We assume work is supposed to be difficult/boring/soul-draining/etc and we accept that as "normal" even though we spend half of our lives in that space! If I were to tell you that you had to spend half of your life in a pit of vipers that tested you at every moment but was a necessary experience in order to enjoy the *other* half of your life, would you accept that or would you question the premise? Every person reading this sentence right now has access to a life history of experiences that played a note, or a song, or a symphony to their soul and, for those that listened and heeded and followed that composition, there lies a calling where work meets life and life meets work, they both fall in love, get married, and exist in tandem playing notes together and finding the best venues and audiences for those artistic works.

> My father!—methinks I see my father.
> O where, my lord?
> In my mind's eye Horatio.
>
> *Hamlet* by William Shakespeare[2]

Close your eyes and think of what you had for breakfast yesterday. Do you SEE it? Try again with the type of dog that lives across the street or the intersection a block or two over from where you live. Do you SEE them? In your mind's eye, of course, but do you *see* them?

Since the first cave paintings to our twenty-first century and 24/7 world of digital media and visual stimuli, we live an increasingly visual world and one where advertisers know what captures our attention in the form of visuals. Nothing tells a STORY like a visual.

Given the rapidly changing climate of our planet, we see more-and-more stories that show the effect weather has on wildlife all over the world. At the present moment, Australia is being gradually and systemically overwhelmed by bushfires that are growing to monumental proportions. While stories claim that 480 million animals are feared to have died and somewhere in the neighborhood of 9.9 million acres have been burned, the best way to convey this environmental tragedy to the rest of the world is through visual images. Images of massive flames and koalas drinking any available water dot the social media landscape. Images like that drive the story and serve the narrative that, in this case, Australia is in trouble! Images serve a purpose that transcends language barriers in the same way music transcends cultures and global regions. Images are how we feel emotion and how we quickly digest information. *The image tells a* ***story***. As the old saying goes, "a picture says a thousand words."

Consider how quickly you can decipher what this shape is called: "*A shape consisting of all points in a plane that are a given distance from a given point.*"[3] Did it take you a minute? The answer, of course, is a circle. Had I instead opted to illustrate a circle shape here, your brain would process and identify that shape 15.4 times faster or in as little as 13 milliseconds than the initial description of the circle shape I provided you.[4] By comparison, the average human blink of an eye is much longer at 100 milliseconds. The name for this concept is the Picture Superiority Effect and it illustrates the core idea that we process information and stories conveyed with images much faster than text alone. Research into the Picture Superiority Effect found that study participants remember a word about 10 percent of the time three days after being told that word. The same participants remember that word *with* an associated image 65 percent of the time three days later.[5]

And our own experiences exemplify these findings. Try describing a photo to someone on the phone versus sharing the actual photo with them. When scrolling through a news feed on social media, do you stop, pause, and read content that has a photo associated with it—something that catches your eye? That is the power of imagery. Imagery is the lifeblood of all designers!

What is your favorite color? Is it blue? Red? Something more specific and less primary? The psychology of color has been one of the least understood and yet most interesting sciences. The power of knowing what color can do and using it in your designs to oh-so-subtly influence your audience is as important as it is fascinating. Allow me to illustrate:

First: think of the last fancy restaurant you went to for a birthday or anniversary dinner perhaps? That ambiance is translated to digits on the check at the end of the meal. How did so many digits get there? Did you have the appetizer ... and some drinks ... and multiple courses ... and the dessert? Other than the food being fantastic and the overall experience being or not being what you hoped it would be, consider some other characteristics of the evening: What was the lighting like? How long did the dinner take start-to-finish? Describe the décor to yourself. The music? The wall color? If these latter questions unrelated to the meal are a little difficult to remember that's the point! The overall goal of the experience for the restauranteur is for you to be there—right there—for the longest possible amount of time to achieve the longest possible number of digits ahead of the decimal point on the bill at the conclusion of that experience. In no way am I saying that the dinner was a con or that the restaurant does not have your experience and, therefore, their reputation and success at the front of their minds, but I am saying that the objective for such an evening is to maximize time and dollars spent over a relatively long period of time. Savoring the experience and coming away from it AS an experience is the goal in that situation and in those circumstances. More often than not, the décor is cool and the lighting relatively soft and dim to the point of almost being dark. Whatever colors you may think of as calming are at play in that environment as well: deep Merlot reds, violets, dark blues, somber earth tones, etc. Just a guess, but I guess I may be close to correct?

Second: picture the last fast-food sandwich shop you entered named after a below-ground network of trains. Have you got that one in your mind? Think about the exchange of goods in that environment versus the fancy restaurant we painted in your mind a moment ago. The design in the fast-food shop is a series of decisions driven by virtually one objective: *speed.* Speed is achieved by way of a rotation of customers through that gastronomic volume of space from the moment you order to the moment you exit—whether you decided to sit down at all on the hard-formed plywood benches they offer for your use. If you take it and go, great. If you eat your sandwich in your car, fine. This particular restaurateur is just fine with that deal for a simple reason: the rate of return they need to equal the amount you spent at the fancy restaurant is inherently tied to the time factor. Move it along. Get your food and get out. Buh-bye. Now what is the primary color in *that* environment? Yellow, yes? Maybe a neon green not found in nature thrown in for good measure, yes? While associated with sunshine, daydreams, and happiness, yellow is actually a harsh color and one that, for a designed environment, is not one that you want to stay inside of too often and for too long. Scientific studies have proven that babies actually cry more in yellow rooms than blue rooms and that yellow can be highly anxiety inducing. But we circle back here to the objective: the purchase of a sandwich and your likely-speedy exit with that sandwich to achieve a consistent rotation of customers in-and-out of the business so that the line never gets too long, and the space never gets too full. And the primary color again? Yellow. You may be cheerful and happy in that space, but you do not want to spend too much time there. That is the point.

Designer as Translator into a Visual Language

Dr. Anna-Charlotte Harvey was a professor of mine in graduate school and a talented scholar on the writings of Swedish and German playwrights. While doing a report on Bertolt Brecht, I stopped her in a hallway with a book I had found in the archives of the library. Always the designer fascinated with the pictures of any book I had in-hand, I reveled at original photographs of Brecht's stage plays capturing important moments in historic productions of world theatre. In showing them to her I lamented that, while I was fascinated by the old photographs, I had no idea what productions I was looking at or what the author was saying about them because the book was written entirely in German. Dr. Harvey paused a moment, pulled the reading glasses she had on the top of her head to her nose, and proceeded to *read the words to me!* I was astonished and felt like a child again hearing words on a page I could not read myself. Dr Harvey was using her expertise to teach. Her knowledge and talents as a translator and her mastery of language were put to immediate use to enlighten me on the marvelous imagery that had captivated me.

Design is an exercise in translation as well. Input followed by output.

Visual Alchemy

The first design project out of the gate for my beginning scenic design students is something called the "Dream Box." Over the years, I have found the exercise can have a profound impact on setting the table for the remainder of the semester for young designers. Consider yourself a system of input stimuli and output product. The designer takes in a play via a script, envisions an environment with others, and the output is a design eventually realized on a stage. The Dream Box involves a similar approach, but the input stimuli come from *within* the designer. The process is simple: student designers are tasked with visualizing a dream (or emotional event if they cannot remember a dream) in three dimensions using the most basic of design elements: color, texture, light, pattern, line, shape, etc. The results are spectacularly beautiful, abstract, and evocative.

The presentation of the dream boxes by students is the best part! The "presenter" says nothing at all. Classmates analyze the dream box for design elements and what they are subliminally telling us. Does the dream involve drowning of some kind or some twisted Escher-esque fantasy of intersecting staircases or some other otherworldly volume of space? Once warmed up, students are coaxed to draw out a narrative or the beginning of a story that describes the dream . . . and all the while, the presenter stays silent. Someone may come close to the dream storyline and the presenter might smile or nod in approval, but the exercise demonstrates the raw beauty of the unspoken visual language that is design. Think of it! Being able to communicate an *entire narrative* with no words at all. What magic! Design is and always has been a communication without words. Completely non-verbal. What a feat of visual alchemy! (See plate 5.)

Taking the dream box to the next level for students involves the simple selection of two words: a noun and an adjective. The process of selecting just two words and then designing *that* supports the idea that the theatrical volume is whatever we want it to be. We have moved from a volume in visual support of our dreams to one born of just two words! (See plate 6.)

My sister is just 15 months younger than I am. During our school years, that often meant a lot of competition and what might pass as hazing on a high school campus. Thankfully, we were one year apart in school, so we were rarely, if ever, in the same class . . . until she was a Junior and I was a Senior. That year, on the first day of class for each of us, I arrived and took a seat in World History. I sauntered in, sat down, and looked across the room to see who I might know. My gaze landed on my sister whom I was stunned to see in the room at all. This had never happened before! Looking across at her, we began a silent conversation. She was in this class. I was in this class. But we both knew that we both could *not* be in this class. That was a given. Reluctantly, I rolled my eyes and in a moment of chivalrous acquiescence I pointed at myself and silently mouthed to her: "I'll go." I approached the teacher's desk and requested a pink slip to switch to another class. At first, the teacher informed me that I would need a valid excuse to be removed from the class and that I would need to cite some kind of worthy accommodation to warrant my leaving the class before it even started. I acknowledged her frustration and simply replied "You don't understand: my *sister* is in this class." The teacher likely ran through a series of mid-semester scenarios and squabbles in her head and immediately decided she'd rather avoid those for sure. She quickly whipped out a pink slip, signed it, and sent me on my way. I spent the better part of five minutes in World History that day and took the only other equivalent option I had in World Geography. Since that day, I've often thought of my life as a game of catch-up on the World History front. I never took it, but one could argue that the rest of my career has been spent studying history in the context of designing plays. And I've loved every minute perhaps because it's all new to me. The content I *should* know resides in my sister's brain after all. The theatre profession allows you this absolutely wonderful and marvelous excuse to fall down research rabbit holes! Think about it: set design is an excuse to study random topics in the context of history. At any given time, I might be researching the hallways of the West Wing during LBJ's first term as President (*All the Way*), the architecture of streets in Amsterdam (*Diary of Anne Frank*), and the fascinating story of two brothers named Collyer who buried themselves under 136 tons of junk in a Harlem brownstone apartment building over a period of about 50 years (*The Dazzle*).

As a designer, images *ARE* your language. You must be a collector, purveyor, and lover of them. You are to be, if you are not already, an expert in your field in the same way Dr. Harvey was an expert in hers. Color, texture, shadow, light, scale, pattern, line, and contrast are to be your language as you combine and collect imagery for every project that may confront you and every show you may tackle as a designer.

These elements are to simultaneously be your catalyst for dialogue about the piece you are designing and your muse for the journey moving forward on the design path. Imagery provokes conversation. If the design for a play is a "jacket" to try on a piece of written work, then each image is a stitch in that proverbial jacket—the building block for the entire wardrobe that is to be the design for the piece. Every member of a design team wields his or her needle as the visual interpreter of the written work.

> Use design as a language for things that are not in our vocabulary.
>
> Idris Mootee[6]

Remember that *this* is *your* language! You are the collector and interpreter for what might be the touchstone image that sets the entire design process on fire. What painting/photo/abstraction might encapsulate the piece in a single and powerful visual image? And what a time to be alive when the ability to

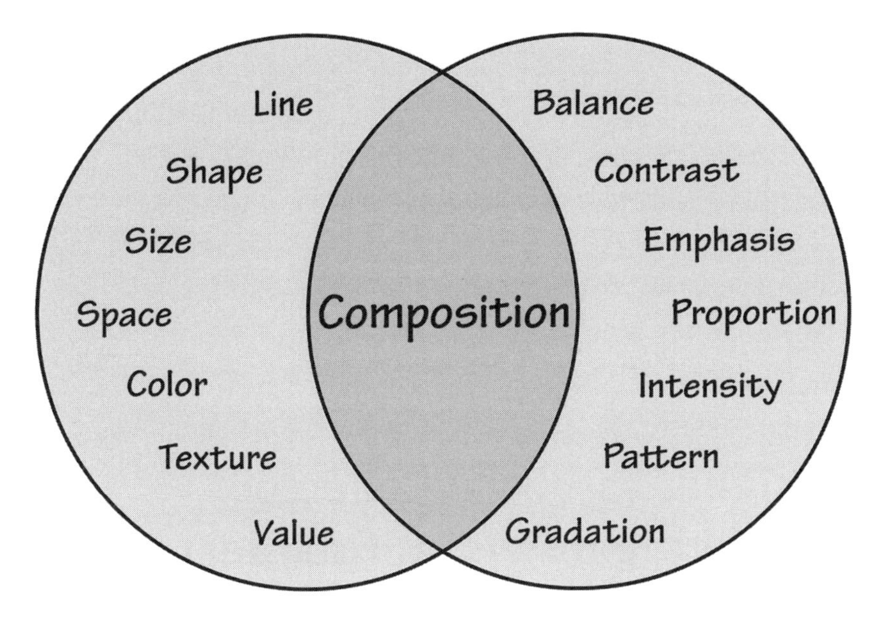

Figure 3.1 Design Elements Diagram. *Source: open source.*

shape and share imagery is so easy in an online world. But remember that the responsibility remains to the piece you are serving; you and your creative teammates are the vehicle for truly and passionately telling that story.

1 If the story is about loss, what does loss LOOK like?
2 If the story is about pain, what does pain LOOK like?
3 If the story is about exuberance, what does exuberance LOOK like?

In a sense, you must accept the role of a visual prophet in these early stages of a design. You must, to the best of your abilities, show a director and your fellow design team members what the jacket might look like before an entire team of production professionals help you shape that idea into a real thing. Does it fit? Does it serve the play, and does it embody the collective vision embraced by the creative team? All important questions to answer. But where to begin?

A series of visual touchstones extracted from a much larger volume of imagery can serve as North Stars for a production design. Take the image cited earlier for the *Twelfth Night* design, for example (see Figure 1.1).

As a touchstone image for the design, the image serves as an emotional response to the play in a visual way—mysterious, romantic, and dreamlike.

As design "fuel" for the duration of the process, the image serves a greater purpose when viewed again later in the process. Like a Fabergé egg, there is more to see the more you look: the image can inform the design team as to the power of silhouette in storytelling, a consideration of using forced perspective as a possible option in the stage design to give an illusion of depth and spur a conversation about adding haze to the air for a scene in the play.

ALL of that from one image ... a visual gift that keeps giving. It is an invitation to a designer to truly analyze an image as a composition of its component parts.

Designer as Visual Collector (Bordering on Visual Hoarder)

The research phase of a design process is a gift for many designers. But so many designers short-change this first and most important phase of the process. Obviously lack of time can play a role in abbreviating this step, but research serves so many important purposes in providing fuel for the length of a design process that can last months or perhaps years. Spend some time developing your visual portfolio "playlist" and you'll always have a well to draw from when researching. Consider your current online music account for a moment. You have a series of favorite artists and the algorithms that drive your catalog learn your tendencies and, as a result, you are offered other artists to listen to that "you might also like." Consider a parallel idea for a moment: your brain is the catalog, and your visual stimuli is your "playlist" of favorites. Now that visual imagery is your language, expanding your mental library to include the full breadth of art, photography, film, and everything in between is your stock-in-trade as a designer.

Picture yourself in the waiting area of your doctor's office or where you get your hair cut. Next to you on a short table are random magazines meant for patients and customers to casually flip through while waiting. For me, whenever I had these downtime moments, I would peruse a magazine and find myself running across different types of imagery by some of the best photographers in the world who, let's face it, are *paid* for their photography. They are good! I can recall thinking "Oh, I really like that texture" or "That color is so intense." Now for the admission of guilt associated with this story: for images I really, really liked and that I felt I just HAD to have, I would whistle or cough while slowly tearing out that page from the magazine, nonchalantly fold it up, and put it in my shirt pocket. That magazine clipping ended up in a crude file folder system I had in a drawer in my apartment/studio. Some files had headings like "textures: interior" while others were labeled "lighting", "architecture", or (my favorite) "magic" which included images that did not seem to quite fit anywhere else.

Before the advent of the internet and image searches online, I found myself on a random weekday night at a local used bookstore or library browsing stacks for research related to a show I was designing. The journey was a bit of a treasure hunt. Go to a card catalog and write down some Dewey decimal system letters and numbers that may—note *may*—be the key to unlocking a great book of visual imagery that will give me a sense of the place I was researching. Not surprisingly, I was a frequent visitor of the N (visual arts), NA (architecture), NC (drawing/design/illustration), and, for good measure, the TR (photography) areas. The process seems entirely outdated now, but it taught me a couple of powerful lessons in the value of hard work in finding just the right image or images for the collection I was amassing to share with a director: be open to discovering visual artists that I did not seek in the first place—the adjacent possible notion applied to books, in essence.

I would write, for example, the number NA 600.528 on a small piece of paper with a tiny golfing pencil and head to the stacks to see what the search might yield. But the process also produced an ancillary benefit unbeknownst to me as I plied through the stacks and scanned the numbers on the bindings of the books: I added favorites to my own visual catalog. The books adjacent to as well as above and below the one I was searching for called out to me. I would draw one almost at random and be exposed to an entirely new world of art … or photography … or design. In my search for Richard Avedon's photography, I would find and peruse a book on Ansel Adams. My quest to find some inspiration from Diego Rivera would result in a discovery of the work of Robert Rauschenberg or vice-versa. In each instance, my visual world and image catalog would widen a bit more. Being a fan of one artist would ultimately lead to the discovery of another. What a marvelous way to spend a weekday evening as a young designer in search of inspiration: hunting for *and* finding more favorites for the "visual playlist" you are compiling for a project and expanding your personal library of artists for your own playlist.

Believe it or not, all images that have ever existed do not all exist on the internet. More and more, I see young designers rely almost exclusively on internet searches and collections. For a moment, think of the library—almost any library—as a real-time immersive experience search engine … and you are the engine. There really is no substitute for the experience of browsing—and I would add again widening your visual palette—in the bookstacks at a local bookstore or library. The adjacent possible becomes more probable when you immerse yourself in this type of environment. The thrill of discovering a new artist or photographer that you then add to your "visual playlist" can happen online, but it is a more visceral experience flipping through the pages of a new-found favorite in the midst of thousands of others.

The point is that I was (and still am) a visual collector. The rationale (perhaps even for stealing magazine images) is simple: if you always refer to your own library of loved images when you are designing a project, you will never end up with an image that you do not like. And sometimes you do! While perhaps harsh, I often refer to this is the "ugly baby" conundrum. A director mentions an artist they like in the context of a play. You look at the work, don't like it, but oblige anyway. Before you know it, you are pinning your entire process and referencing the same (hated) art for the six months prior to a show opening. The ugly baby. You are stuck with it. And it is not fun. But I digress …

The compendium of research in those former magazine clippings and now digital files are additional stitches to the design jacket for the project you are designing. At a later date, when I had a play in mind that I was tasked with designing, I would flip through those files, pull out an image, and ask myself:

1 Does this image fit this play?
2 Does it evoke a world we are trying to design?
3 Does it somehow/someway *feel* like the play?

These days, the process is the same but updated using modern tools of course: the cell phone replaces the destruction of doctor's office magazines and files are now entirely digital … but I still have one labeled "Magic" where all the magical imagery (whatever that means) goes.

Get your Inspiration from ANYwhere!

Obviously, this process needs to continually happen when you are NOT designing. Be a visual collector when you are not up against the clock with a deadline, but instead when you are walking to school or the grocery store. If you are awestruck by the quiet beauty of a sunset, take a picture of it. When the architectural detail of an archway you've passed through dozens of times or the pattern of a carpet you've constantly walked on strikes you as worthy of your personal visual collection, take a photo of it. If a texture/color/ magical visual cries out to you to be captured, capture it, embrace it, appreciate it, and curate it into your own personal library of inspiration. That library will consistently remind you that you are a designer. Your aesthetic—your designer DNA—is contained in those files. Those files become your wellspring of imagination and curiosity. Those files are a reason to tout, even if only to yourself, the hard evidence as to your "eye" as a designer. Perhaps even the reason you chose to design at all. Those images exist as the result of shining opportunities when you had to find visual inspiration and the time you took to explore for explorations sake!

I had an opportunity in 2004 to design a brand-new play called *Subject Tonight Is Love* at the Alliance Theatre Company in Atlanta, Georgia. The play is a moving story about three generations of family members dealing with Alzheimer's disease. It stars a character named Ruby who we see get progressively worse in terms of her condition throughout the play as she battles the disease. By the end, she barely recognizes her own daughter Diana or grandson, Josh. The piece is very episodic in nature with several locations that shift from one to another at an almost frenetic pace. A half-page phone call is followed by a quick shift to a hospital room for another page of dialogue followed by a quick flashback to an earlier mother/daughter moment. The result is a solemn and emotional journey which highlights the multi-generational layers of complexity that affect an entire family when one beloved family member suffers from Alzheimer's. Many audience members see themselves in the characters and feel the pain they feel as the disease progresses, and the play draws to a close.

The piece is written by playwright and friend Sandra Deer who wrote the play as a kind of autobiographical homage to her late mother who suffered and eventually died from the disease. The play ends with a bittersweet scene between Ruby and her daughter Diana in a hospital room where Diana delivers her final goodbye to her mother (see plate 7).

During the technical rehearsals, I happened to seat myself next to Sandra for a moment when we were working on cues onstage for the final scene. As most of my design and production work at that point was behind me, I wanted to know if we had "done her proud" with what was a very personal story for her debuting onstage in a matter of days. Curious if our production did her play justice, I turned to her and asked, "Is this truly your story onstage here?" She politely turned to me and whispered: "Everything except this scene. I never got to have this scene with my own Mom." The play was a dramatic eulogy to her. As a designer, how do you not feel a sense of responsibility to her memory and that story?

Responsibility to the Story as a Storyteller

Oft overlooked in the maddening push to meet design deadlines, share sketches, and relate ideas is that each play is a profound responsibility to the story we are collectively telling. An effort should always be made to first realize and then accept that producing a play is a vital breathing of life into a story born, written, and sculpted into shape with love by a solitary artist we call a playwright. They may not be in the room with us. They may never see their play performed and produced. But each story is, by varying degrees, an extension of that person's psyche and self. Care and effort must be taken to serve that story nobly with reverence and honor. Without it, there is no structure whatsoever to the production being designed. The success of the storytelling drives it all.

With this level of artistic reverence in mind, consider these mantras when designing:

1. *You cannot Google image search your way through design research.* Do yourself a favor and do the *work* of searching—and from all kinds of sources: magazines, books, your own photography, the internet, and all of life. Take the time necessary to serve the story.
2. *Be a "visual collector"* as often as possible to fuel the success of individual projects that draw from that collection. Snap photos and curate them into files that make sense to you. Files on textures, color, and magic will slowly grow to become a wealth of visual resources for you and "stitches in the jacket" of your design. Dipping into those files will be like a walk into visual worlds that you truly look forward to seeing again. Some images are "old friends" that perhaps served an important purpose on an earlier design and others are new additions that join the cacophony of imagery you've collected. This is YOUR well that you go to for a reminder of your aesthetic "eye." Balance the love of those images with the need to find ones that properly fit the play you have in mind and the resource will always give back to you in spades.

3 *Never be satisfied*: sometimes hundreds of images may yield just a few "touchstone" images that are those visual "North Stars" for you. Finding those good ones often means tossing out a hundred of other bad ones.

Some years ago, a pro football coach by the name of Bill Parcells imparted some wisdom to his young quarterback Tony Romo. He simply said: "Never let 'good enough', be good enough."[7] The path towards pursuing a unique or thoughtful design begins with a discussion of the world and a deep dive into the research. Like the *Indiana Jones* series of films, finding just one true touchstone image can—and should—be a journey. If it is not, something is missing. Some other influential images are still out there. Find them! You have perhaps heard artists lament when something is "too easy." There exists a feeling that, while you have some experience designing, landing on a concept based on easily found and hastily discovered imagery can lead to that type of feeling: that it was just "too easy." Continuing to search for those influential touchstone images means it must be a journey. It must be a bit like discovering the holy grail amongst thousands of holy grail "imposters." DO the work. It WILL pay off. Trust the method and you will begin to trust your own "designer eyes."

> There may be said to be two classes of people in the world; those who constantly divide the people of the world into two classes, and those who do not.
>
> Robert Benchley[8]

At times, I am reminded of a quote above when I attempt to divide *something* into two parts of *anything*. It serves as a bit of an intellectual hiccup that stops me from assuming that the world is really that black-and-white as to reduce anything into just two types.

It is important in this research phase of the process to consider exactly what you are seeking when perusing bookstacks and online compendiums of imagery. As a general rule and one I ask of my own students, I think research for any project being designed should include equal parts of research from two buckets: the literal and abstract. Put another way: the "looks" and the "feels." Both buckets feed off of each other.

For reasons too embarrassing to reveal, I was briefly hospitalized one night and spent hours and hours in hospital emergency rooms and exam rooms (see plate 8).

I think I finally went home at around 3am. At one point during that epic evening, I recalled that while researching the last play I did with scenes in a hospital room, I had difficulty truly finding accurate imagery of what those really look like from color to equipment to lighting. With advancements in hospital technology on an almost constant basis, an increase in patient privacy over the years, and the simple fact that taking photos inside a space meant for the sick is simply not what people think of doing, I was not at all surprised that finding accurate photos of modern-day hospital rooms was a challenge. So, at what was probably around 2am or so, I stood up and snapped this photo. A bit of a morbid thought to have, but I knew I would not get the opportunity again (or at least I hoped I would not be back there for a while). I cannot quite tell you what made me think of it at the time, but I knew I would regret it if I didn't make a visual note of that night in the hospital and come away with at least one useful piece of research. I was doing a bit of visual collecting that night. How that room looked still reminds me of how the experience felt. "Looks and feels." The image has a dialogue with me—a memory of that moment.

Research is your fuel for the long journey of a design from answering questions that range from "What is the world?" to "What's the shine on the floor?" You can never have too much of it.

Identifying Patterns

Images have an important dialogue with each other as well. What each piece of art says to you, the viewer, has importance, but what multiple pieces say *to each other* can lead to some wonderful and provocative conversations in a design meeting. Phrases along the lines of "this piece looks like the world we are in and this piece feels like the world we are in" begin to pop-up. The conversation that started with the if/then has now moved on to include a visual language and a probing of some thematic and conceptual depths of the piece.

One obvious and important key is that you must be analyzing pieces of research next to each other! Consider sharing a slideshow of research imagery one-by-one like a deck of cards: first one, then the next, then the next. No relationships *across* that imagery can ever come to pass in that format because we are not seeing the images as they relate to one another. We may remember that image #1 had a blue hue to it when we get to image #25, but that is unlikely. Some of the most productive design conversations I have had in my career are provoked by the simplest of gestures: scattering a ton of printed/pulled/stolen images out on a literal table and finding which ones "rise to the top" as touchstone images that speak a visual language related to the play (see plate 9).

Relationships between images are important windows into how the play feels to us and, eventually, our audience. I require my own students to share visual collages of research and have banned the one-by-one reveal of research in class.

It is in research collages like these that one can begin to see themes, but also examine relationships across different pieces. We begin to see how light and color will serve an important purpose in the design of this play. We begin to analyze and compare textures and surfaces in another. Perhaps most importantly, we can begin to translate this first baby-step of the design and "make hope visible" for what the design can look like in the end.

Identify your "Cup of Tea" . . . and Ignore That

Be wary of what is your "cup of tea" visually. Remember that your design is not a design for your hospital room or bedroom or play environment. Your design is for the environment occupied by your characters in your play. There is a big difference and it is wise to recognize it. Theatre design and interior design vary in this respect. In the former, we are tasked with creating environments that are reflections of the characters who occupy those environments. In the latter, interior designers are compensated for their own personal designer eye and unique aesthetic. Of course, they take their client's needs and desires into account when designing, but the client hired that interior designer because they want that aesthetic, that style, that flavor applied to their home or business.

While in graduate school, I had a marvelous and unique opportunity to participate in a juried exhibition to a stellar group of panelists that included designers Ming Cho Lee, Peter Maradudin, and Beeb Salzer, playwright Edward Albee, costume designer Patricia Zipprodt, critic Martin Bernheimer, and artistic director Martin Benson. The entire experience was as nerve-wracking as you might expect given the assemblage of legendary theatrical talent in the room at that moment. For the sports fan, an equivalent might be a chance to shoot hoops with Michael Jordan, Lebron James, and Larry Bird watching you do it.

Three teams of designers, actors, and a director presented a short scene and full designs for *The Miser* by Molière to this dream team jury of artists assembled before us in the front row of a theatre. At one point famed Broadway costume designer Patricia Zipprodt was asked a simple question by a classmate as it related to their approach to designing costumes for the play: How do you design costumes for a contemporary play? Zipprodt's answer was as elegant as it was profound: "I think of the character, I go to their closet, and I pick something out."[9]

The design of a play is not about choosing what *you* want from a selection in *your* closet to put on *your* set. Designing is about digging deep and with empathy into the characters that occupy the world. What would *they* choose to wear, sit on, live in, etc? That is the question.

Some years later, I designed a production of a play called *Jesus Hates Me* by Wayne Lemon. Wayne is a friend and son of a Baptist preacher. The piece is about a character named Ethan who is a twenty-something former Texas football prodigy whose promising career and prospects he had in the sport vanished following a career-ending injury. The primary setting is the seventeenth hole of a Bible-themed miniature golf course in Texas called "Blood of the Lamb" where Ethan is forced to pick up the pieces of his post-football life while living with his mother who is also the proprietor of the bizarre golf course in a tiny Airstream trailer on the property. The play is about Ethan and his story, but his inner conflict is driven, in part, by his current situation: living with his Mom in a trailer where any possible escape out of that environment leads to dead ends for him. He is *in conflict with* his environment. This particular "jacket" does not fit him—and shouldn't! The audience should both hear and see that struggle. The space—the proverbial jacket here—actually belongs to his mother and represents the equivalent of a straitjacket for Ethan. He struggles against it violently as it represents what is left of his aspirations for fame on the gridiron. While Ethan in this context may actually be wearing what came from the character's closet referred to by Zipprodt, the space should serve as one of a number of protagonists with whom Ethan is wrestling in his life.

With the "check yourself and your cup of tea" point made during this early research phase; another very important point surfaces that cannot be overstated. In this age of on-demand access to anything and everything online from the latest statement from a celebrity just a few seconds old to 3D recreations of the Parthenon from Ancient Greece, there is a temptation that you have likely experienced in answer to a question that you have likely asked yourself as a young designer: "I'm designing play X, so I wonder how others have designed play X in the past?" Please, *please* resist this urge to look, check, or to even peek at another design for the same piece that you are currently designing! It is not hyperbole to say that it is poison. It muddies the water so much and is an image that sometimes remains embedded in your psyche and therefore your process for the duration of the design and implementation of your ideas. Consider what a quick peek will do on so many levels:

- It will embed itself in your brain as a perhaps perceived "correct" way to the design the piece. There is NO correct way. There is only your way that is a unique recipe for the unique team of artist ingredients you have on that creative team.
- The above can fester into a destructive inner monologue that grows into a pariah for your own creative process that ranges from self-doubt of your own abilities and talents to a full-blown case of imposter syndrome where you may believe that you are faking the entire designer title you have bestowed—and rightfully owned—on yourself. You may experience yourself muttering "I am a designer, but I'm not (blank) designer . . . and never will be."
- Perusing old designs for the same play is not a way to breathe life into a piece for your current audience. Today's audience has new and different perspectives than an audience that witnessed the same play ten, twenty, or fifty years ago. The design process is not a recipe; the challenge is not to find secret ingredients to put in it. It reflects an artistic work meant to say something slightly different to a modern audience than it did when it first debuted, no matter how recently that debut happened. Know as well that the Samuel French scripts that exist for plays have meticulous stage directions, a tiny groundplan, and prop lists because those plays were published with the stage manager's script—not the playwright's. Ignore them. Remove them.
- Why dig in that part of the garden anyway? You will not find what you seek there! The design is an *interpretation* of an environment and not the environment. That design represents a different process with a different creative team.

Primary and Secondary Research

With a few exceptions, the vast majority of all visual imagery of any kind has been edited in some way. From photographs online and in texts to impressionist paintings in the Louvre, there exists a filter like the layers in a

Photoshop file that are placed between you and the uncropped, unedited, unmanipulated, and unaltered original. What was once a complex image editing process performed by only a few artists and designers in front of equipment few of us even had access to is now a tool that fits comfortably in the palm of your hand that can twist, tweak, and twirl an image into something entirely unrecognizable from its original form. Every tweak is a filter and (again) an *interpretation* of that image into one that satisfies the artist as editor. All images that fall into this extremely vast category are considered secondary research. For a designer, research of this kind can prove very valuable and applicable to a design process. Artistic conversations of enormous depth can rise from a "look how this artist interpreted this environment" and can lead to some marvelous adaptations and interpretations of your own unique to you and your collaborative process with fellow artists.

But that type of visual research is not primary research. Primary research is, to use an earlier example, the photo of the hospital exam room that I took myself and lived and experienced (for far too many hours) myself. A designer in that realm realizes and recognizes that he or she is that visual collector at that moment with a need to document that moment as a piece of primary research for prosperity purposes. You can be assured that primary research has no filters of any kind obscuring the original unaltered image. It is yours. You took it. You *lived* it.

A trip to St Louis for a project in 2008 prompted me to take advantage of the visit to research another project that I was working on at the time: a design for *Glass Menagerie* by St Louis native Tennessee Williams. The play is written about a time in Tennessee's life when he lived with his mother and sister in a cramped St Louis apartment from about 1936 to 1938. Tom is the lead character and chief narrator for what is an autobiographical story about Tennessee's own upbringing in St Louis. Like Ethan's character from *Jesus Hates Me*, Tom is at odds with his environment and struggles with his deep desire to run far away from St Louis versus his familial obligation as the sole breadwinner of the family. Like Ethan, he's trapped.

But long before the design saw the light of day, I decided to take advantage of the trip to St Louis to fashion my own walking tour of Tennessee's own neighborhood and walk a mile in his shoes seventy years later. Like my hospital experience, I did not want to let the opportunity to experience the research pass me by. I wanted to get a sense of the place firsthand and attempt to survey what amounts to a historical landmark in the annals of American theatre history. Eager for my self-guided Tennessee tour, I signed up for a couple of hours with the company car and headed off to 4633 Westminster

Place: one of two St Louis boyhood homes for Tennessee Williams. Without access to the apartment itself (now an Airbnb), I was intent on at least getting a good look at the fire escape where multiple scenes in the play take place. I even took my students there once to underline the importance of exploring primary research (see plate 10).

For a non-St Louisan, one is struck by the enormity of what amounted to canyons flanked by brick walls to either side and small windows of light between them—an idea that later served as a metaphor for Tom's situation. It served as a visual element in the design in an attempt to subtly suggest his inability to reach those windows of light and the freedom they represented to him. Helpless. Powerless. Trapped. (See plate 11.)

Real primary research means going to uncomfortable places to immerse yourself in the world to the degree that it is possible to do so. It requires a number of extra steps when, as we all know, typing a word or words into an online search is a lot easier. But in hindsight, the experience made for a better connection and a deeper sense of place than I could ever find in hours of research online. And I am not going to lie—it was kind of a thrill. Wayfinding through a project means giving yourself the best chance to do well in that project. Being able to come back to the team and say "I did this thing where I walked down some alleys and I shot all these photos and the fire-escape he wrote about faces North and this and that"—I mean—is there anything better than telling a good story to friends who are on that journey with you to create a world for storytelling and transport an audience to 1930s St Louis?

I was trying to convey the "go the extra mile" with your research lesson to my design students at UC-Berkeley one semester. The play they were designing was *The Subject Tonight is Love* by Sandra Deer—the beloved play about Alzheimer's. In what only a designer may define as a "stroke of luck," I located an Alzheimer's Day Clinic near campus and arranged for students to spend time with Alzheimer's patients. The staff there helped us to a room where chairs were arranged in a large circle with an alternating pattern of students and patients wrapping around the room—one patient sitting between two students and so forth around the space. After being seated, a member of the staff introduced a large coffee can with slips of paper. Each slip of paper was a simple question prompt along the lines of "Do you recall if your father ever had a mustache?" or "Do you remember playing an instrument?" Both students and patients methodically chose one slip of paper, read it aloud, and answered the question. For the patients, the exercise proved worthwhile in maintaining their memories, but it is difficult to overestimate the profound impact it had on the students. One patient was seemingly transported to a time when she was no older than the students seated around her as she regaled us with a tale of being a flapper in 1920s Chicago. She touted that she was quite a dancer "in those days" to the collective amazement of the students. When the experience was over, I had students who wanted to stay for the rest of the day. They were smitten and deeply moved by our class that day. The main character, Ruby, came alive for them that day in the form of about fifteen patients at an Alzheimer's Day Clinic. After that day, they viewed their assignment to design the play in an entirely different way imbued with a deep sense of responsibility to the patients in that room. Ruby's story was *their* story too. To not pour their heart-and-soul into the design would mean that they were somehow betraying their new friends and surrogate grandparents at the clinic.

Staging a play is a pact with the story and a bond with the content of that story. To be so expeditious in your process that you ignore that one simple fact will not necessarily mean that the production suffers or that the audience will hate it. It may, but that's not likely. What it does mean is that the design job can quickly begin to feel more and more like a job. Clock in/clock out. Rinse-and-repeat. The gravity, meaning, and purpose may be gone.

But people have been gracious enough to believe in you!

A much more meaningful research design process contains frequent moments when you recognize that you are a designer and, by that definition, you are afforded the *opportunity* (not duty) to explore the research on a level that goes beyond the obvious avenues for obtaining it.

You get to (you don't have to) explore a topic on a deeper level and call it your job.

You get to research political movements and historical characters and global societies.

You get to share those findings with people on the same journey as you.

You get to plumb the depths of a story in hopes of manifesting that story onstage in a believable and transformative way for an audience of strangers you've never met.

And when you get to do *that* and call it your *job*—don't "let good enough be good enough."

4

Clawing and Scratching Out an Idea

Chapter Outline

Design is Messy . . . and Lose the Boxes

I have design students that come from an architecture background who do amazingly beautiful work in that class. They research and craft a beautiful model, light it, photograph it, and display it proudly to their peers. In those instances, I often say something along the lines of "please, you must put this in your portfolio!—it is beautiful" and the response I often get is something along the lines of "but my portfolio is for *architecture*." Herein lies the artificiality of the division divide. Students—and many adults to be honest—feel that one

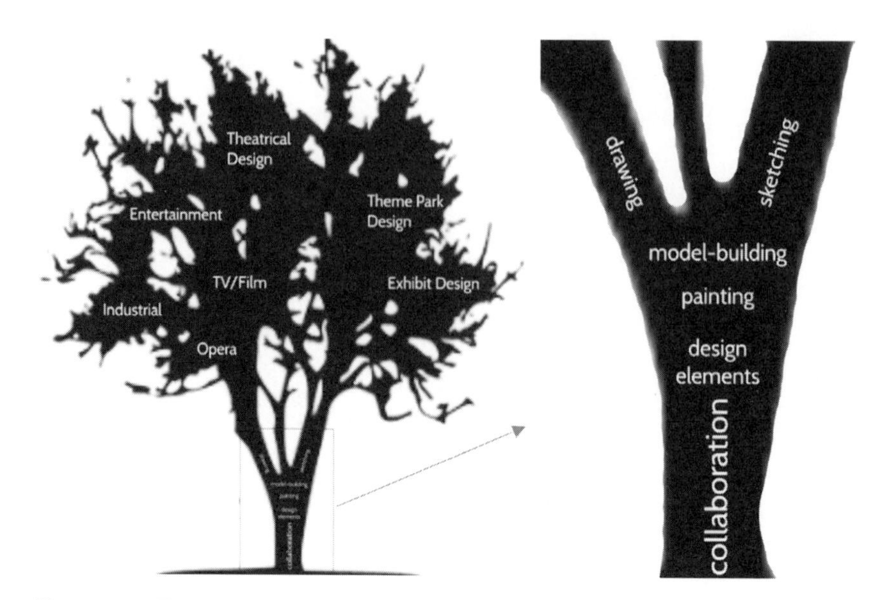

Figure 4.1 The "Design Tree". *Source: graphic by author.*

type of art (architecture) cannot possibly accept another avenue of artistic content (set design) into it because it "doesn't fit" into that box. It is not "meant" for that box. My argument takes a step back to ask: "Why do we need a box at all?" Why do we think that we cannot ourselves crossover into different mediums of expression from the "trunk" of the design tree?

Designers who master the fundamentals within the "trunk" of this design tree can find themselves in different branches of the same tree with very little effort. My own career is an example of this phenomenon. From the theatre design world, I have done work in exhibit and theme park design . . . both branches of the same design tree. Colleagues have leveraged a degree in theatrical lighting design to foray into concert and architectural lighting . . . both branches of the same design tree.

Artists of all stripes are exploring ways to cross over into other artistic artforms and not to (necessarily) capitalize on one artform or another, but to keep things interesting and pushing their own artistic envelope into other mediums and other forms of creative expression.

- Comedians like Robin Williams became an Oscar-winning actor after and during a life in comedy.
- Artists like David Hockney have become opera set designers.
- Actors like Clint Eastwood become Oscar-winning directors of films.
- And designers (like this one) try to become authors.

Plate 1 Author as a child puppeteer. *Source: photo by author.*

Plate 2 Children playing with pots & pans. *Source: iStock photo via PeopleImages ID: 505657693.*

Plate 3 *Twelfth Night* at University of Washington. *Source: photo by author.*

Plate 4 Rectangular vs round table configurations. *Source: iStock photo and Media Bakery.*

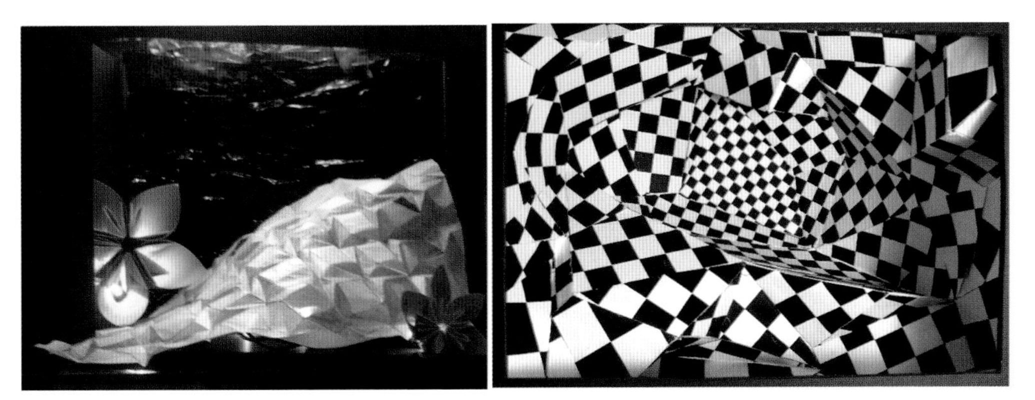

Plate 5 Dream boxes by student designers Jaclyn Casper (left) and Leora Baum (right). *Source: permission from students.*

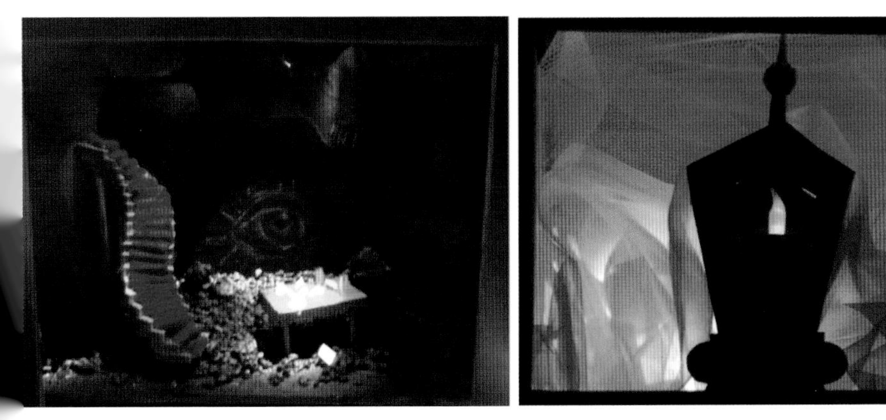

Plate 6 Examples of two words projects by student designers: "Dark Philosophy" by Zoe Morris (left) and "Blushing Belief" by John Craig (right). *Source: permission from students.*

Plate 7 *Subject Tonight is Love* at the Alliance Theatre (design by Robert Mark Morgan). *Source: photo by author.*

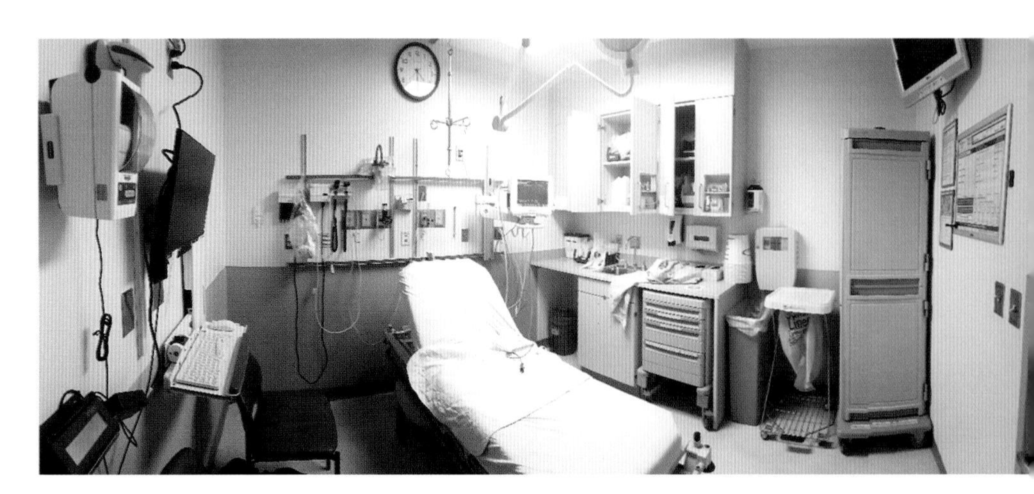

Plate 8 Panoramic photo of a hospital exam room. *Source: photo by author.*

Plate 9 Examples of a digital research collages by students Corinna Siu (left) and Zoe Morris (right) for the same play. *Source: permission of students.*

Plate 10 Design students on the fire escape of Tennessee Williams' former apartment in St. Louis. *Source: photo by author.*

Plate 11 Side-by-side of research and finished design for *Glass Menagerie* at Cleveland Play House. *Source: photos by author.*

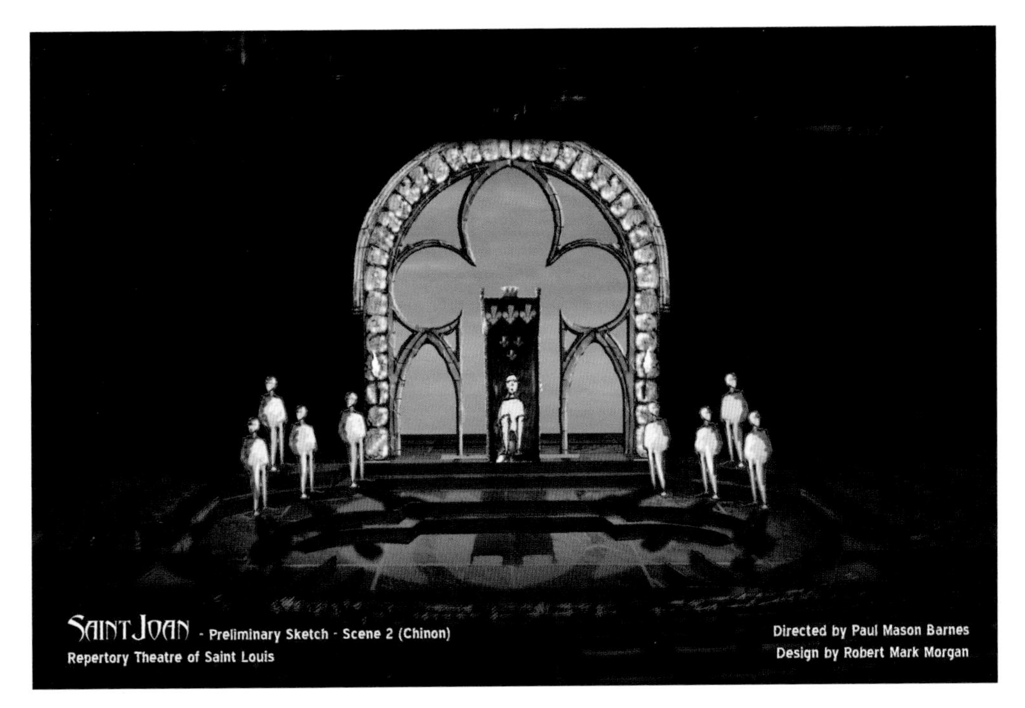

Plate 12 Initial design for *Saint Joan* at the Repertory Theatre of St. Louis.
Source: design by author.

Plate 13 SeaWorld Intensity Games scale model. *Source: photo/design by author.*

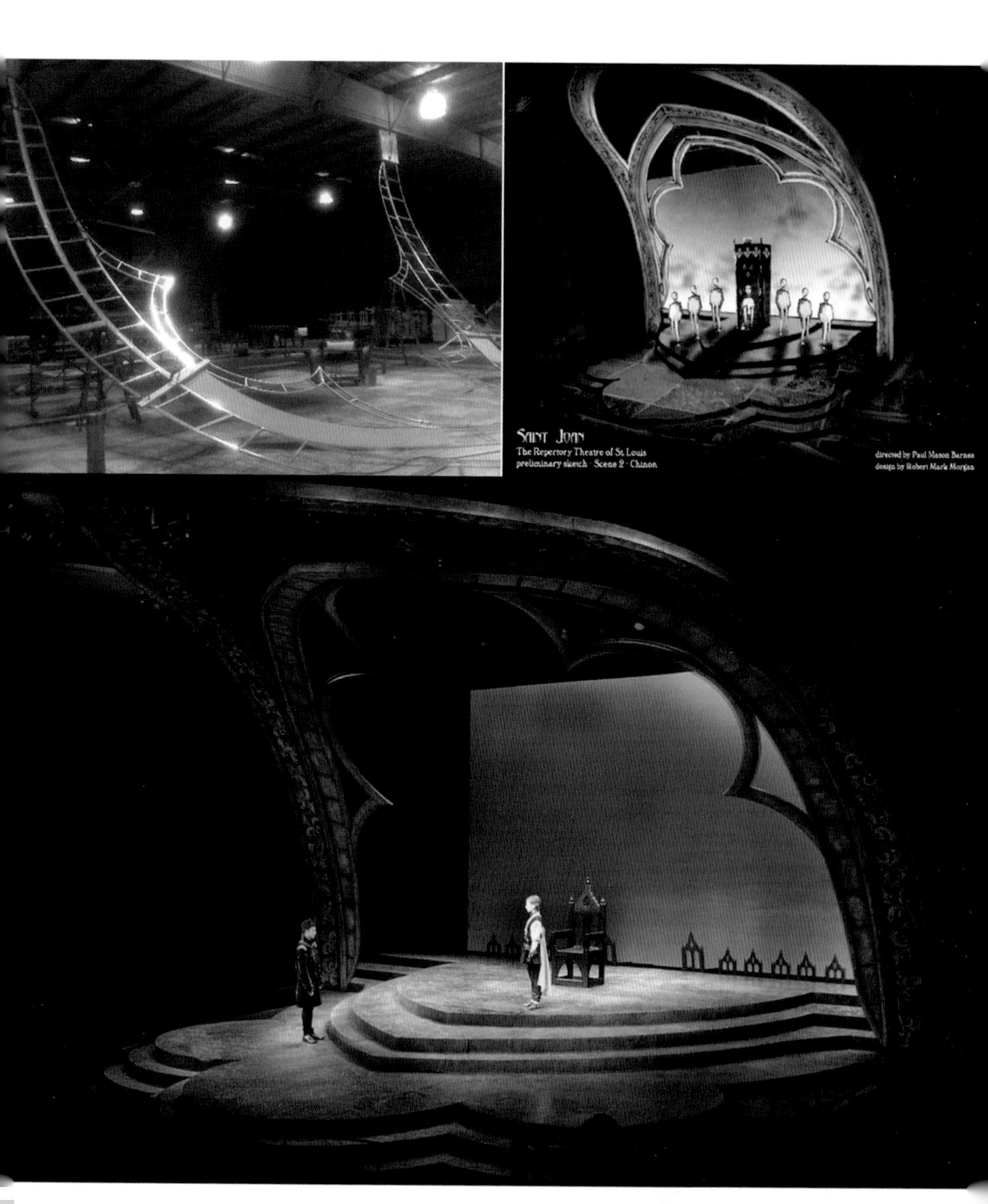

late 14 Design, build, and finished design of *Saint Joan* at the Repertory heatre of St. Louis. *Source: photos/designs by author.*

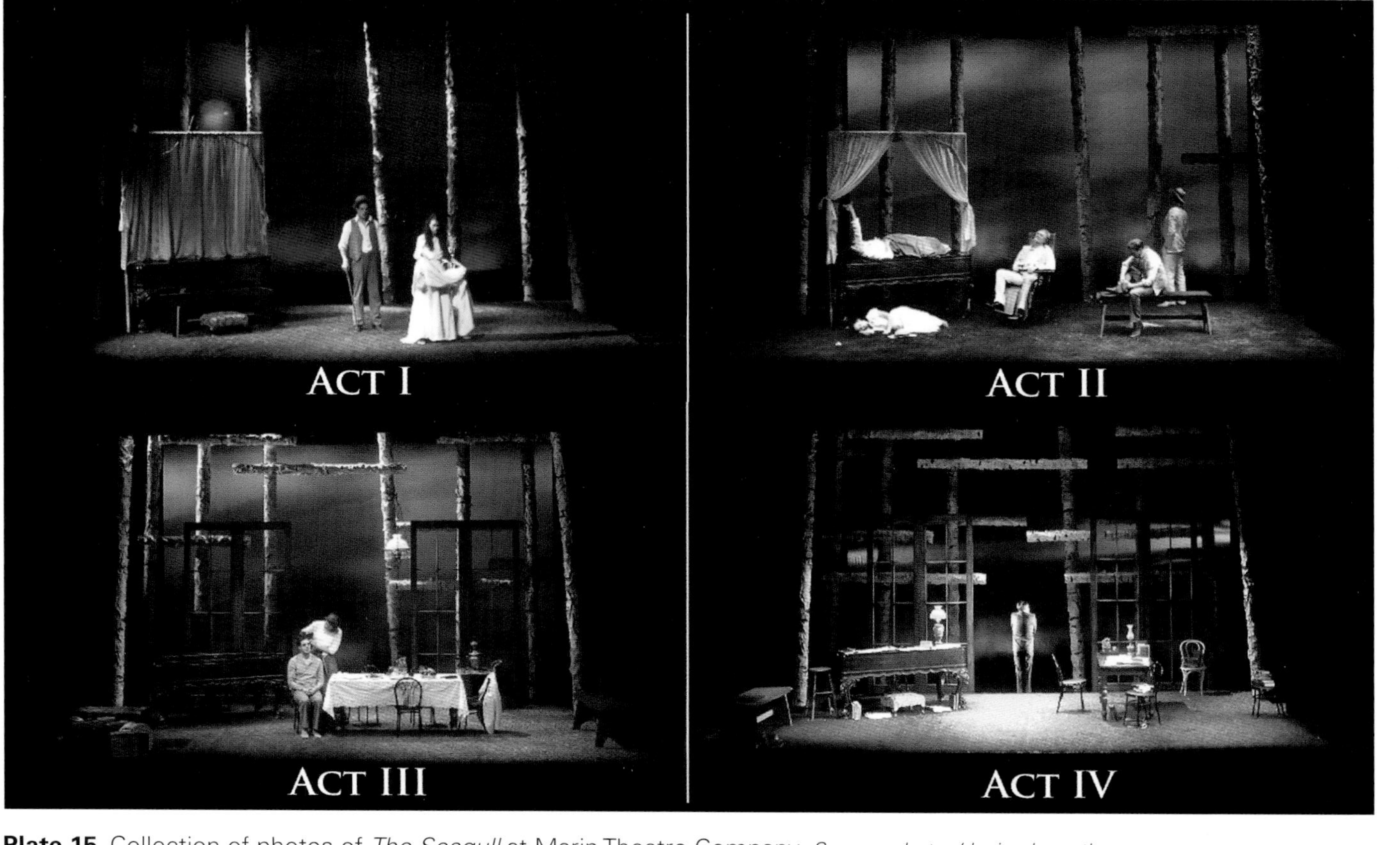

Plate 15 Collection of photos of *The Seagull* at Marin Theatre Company. *Source: photos/design by author.*

Plate 16 *Wizard of Oz* painted backdrop (top) and *Les Misérables* painted backdrop in process (bottom). *Source: photos by author.*

Plate 17 The secret behind the magic of the *The Seagull* (pictured: Jeff Klein). *Source: photo by author.*

Plate 18 Papasan chair frame covered in rafia skirts for "Nest" for Horton-the-Elephant. *Source: photo by author*

Plate 19 Finished design for Act III, Scene 2 of *Major Barbara* at San José Repertory Theatre. *Source: photo by author.*

Plate 20 Photo of present-day ACT Geary Theatre. *Source: ACT archives.*

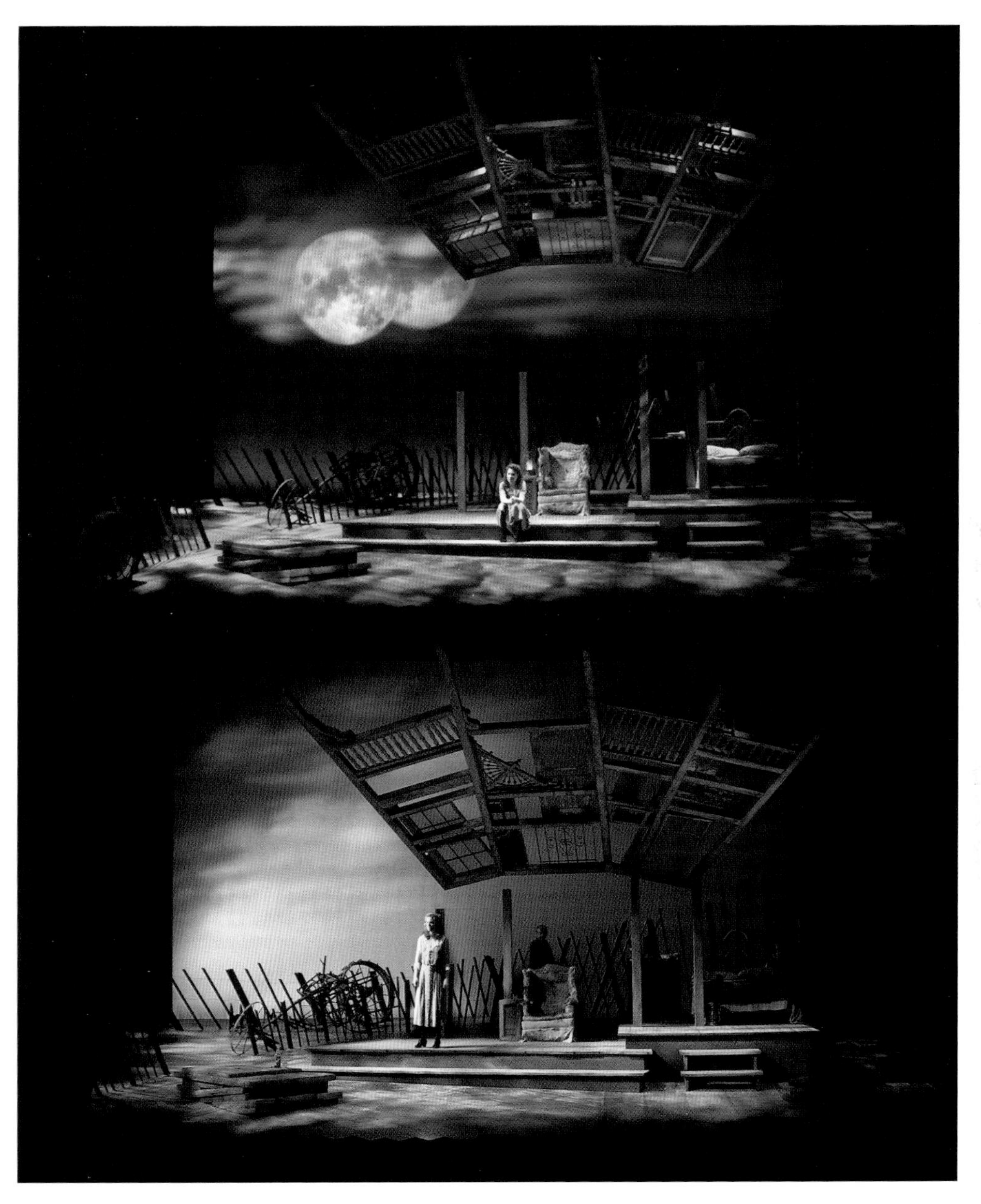

Plate 21 Finished design photos of *A Moon for the Misbegotten* at ACT—San Francisco. *Source: design/photos by author.*

Plate 22 A 3D model imported via augmented reality (AR) on the author's table. *Source: author.*

Plate 23 Screen captures from FrameVR spaces used for theatre (top) and teaching (bottom). *Source: author.*

Plate 24 Choreography by Car Headlights by Jacob Jonas (photo by Matthew Brush). *Source: Matthew Brush.*

Plate 25 Pageant wagon production by Washington University in St. Louis, Spring 2021. *Source: design/photo by author.*

The point is that boxes rarely, if ever, exist in artforms both within them and between them. To be better aware of design opportunities for this type of disruption and reframing of understood norms and systems, Bruce Mau has devised a running-list he calls *An Incomplete Manifesto for Growth* which includes mantras and reminders for recognizing opportunities in redesign. A few favorites:

> "*Love your experiments (as you would an ugly child).* Joy is the engine of growth. Exploit the liberty in casting your work as beautiful experiments, iterations, attempts, trials, and errors. Take the long view, and allow yourself the fun of failure every day."[1]
>
> "*Capture accidents.* The wrong answer is the right answer in search of a different question. Collect wrong answers as part of the process. Ask different questions."[2]
>
> "*Ask stupid questions.* Growth is fueled by desire and innocence. Assess the answer, not the question. Imagine learning throughout your life at the rate of an infant."[3]

Get Lost in the Woods

To get back to the journey of the artist and the worthwhile nature OF that journey, Mau has a mantra for that too. In a 2011 interview, Mau discusses the Center for Massive Change and the importance of iterative practice to explore possibilities in design with what he calls an entrepreneurial mindset. In the same way the Johnny Cash example affords us an opportunity to "get lost" and discover a new way to portray a character, Mau considers a similar journey as it relates to the Center. In his words, we need to "get lost in the forest":

> It's not the content of the experience that you need to learn, it's the experience of the content. It's the experience that you need to learn. You need to know that you can be lost in the forest and find your way out . . . we thought about calling it The Lost in the Forest Institute. There's a difference between being on a picnic and being lost in the forest. When you are on a picnic, you might be in the very same place, but on a picnic you don't care very much about the environment you are in, your concern is about who brought the coke, and who's got the sandwiches. When you are lost in the forest, every piece of information is important to you. The fact that the land slopes this way, and the sun is over there, and I can hear water: all of that information is immediately relevant. That's what an entrepreneur does. An entrepreneur

> processes everything, all l the information as tools. An entrepreneur looks at the landscape looks at the situation and says "you know what? I can use these 3 things and put them together to make a new thing that people really need.[4]

As you know from Chapter 1, if you are reading this book, I am calling you and everyone around you a designer. With this terminology, we *all* can affect change and create disruption (good and bad) in our world that we are co-designing with everyone else on the planet. To be a young designer of any kind and one that can affect positive change, create creative work, and expand the breadth of the questions we ask ourselves about a piece of work we are adapting for the stage, we MUST do all the things that colleagues from Amster to Mau advocate: we must get "lost in the woods!"

Perhaps you've heard the term "do something that scares you every day." Intentionally getting yourself lost in the woods with an idea means YOU catalyze and create the artistic journey. Expanding and pushing the envelope on what you can create means ... getting lost once in a while. Repeat after me:

EVERY ARTIST DOES THIS. YOU ARE NOT THE ONLY ONE.

Musician Leonard Cohen is quoted as saying "If I knew where the good songs came from, I'd go there more often."[5] He struggled with finding his creative muse.

Architect Frank Gehry often finds himself at odds with the sculptural building he is crafting in model form, so he advises himself and his assistant to "be bothered by it" and let it gnaw at them until they figure out what's wrong and follow the next elusive opportunity.[6]

Like the blues singer looking to make a deal with the devil at the crossroads in exchange for an ability to play the guitar like no other, true creativity can be elusive. But the JOURNEY is the thing. While to a different destination surely, the journey for any musician, artist, architect, designer, etc. remains the same. We ALWAYS get "lost in the woods."

Across Space and Time

Another hat I wear in my life is that of a director of an interdisciplinary program called Beyond Boundaries. The basic "why" behind the program is to provide a vehicle for students to answer challenging societal questions without the restrictions of divisional boundaries. An ideal student in the program is one who exemplifies a true divergent thinker and who knows that answering their "big question" will require interdisciplinary study of two or more disciplines and divisions.

But what I must preach in the context of this text on design instruction is more about boundaries than the elimination of them entirely. In my work, I have always found that two sets of boundaries are ever and always tantamount to being a designer: space and time.

Space

Virtually every space I have ever occupied since calling myself a designer at 18 has had a portion of it devoted to the craft. To some that may seem obvious, to others perhaps less crucial but looking back I think the (perhaps tiny) venue that I created for myself in a space that I could call my own "studio" went a long way to legitimizing to others, but more importantly, to myself, that I was a designer. Consider it a testament or flag planted in the ground of your career that unequivocally states to all who might ask you: I am a designer. It may not be full time. I may be only scraping by in the design world. I may have a "day job" that pays the bills, but one drafting-table-size plot of earth that says "this is mine, this is my space to create" can make all the difference and perhaps even serve as your own personal North Star or your own personal nameplate that states with confidence that you are an artist.

Consider a few of my own design "studios":

1. I lived in a "garden level" studio apartment in Minneapolis while working for a children's theatre company as a "Draftsperson/Carpenter/Welder" (the actual title). I got the job knowing just two of those three skills. I lived in a space so tiny that I would hit my head on the drafting table if I woke up too quickly from a nightmare or a sudden sound. Car headlights would shine constantly into my tiny basement apartment and, on one occasion, a car fire in the parking lot nearly melted my garden-level windows.
2. While in Graduate School in San Diego, I lived in a rental house near campus with a small 4x8 shed in the backyard amongst the anise growing wild. That tiny shed became my studio where I would spend hours crafting models and doing drawings. More than once, bugs would land in the model that I was photographing in a way that made them in-scale appear twelve feet long! I would pass the time listening to a tiny black-and-white television with an antenna made from aluminum foil. On Monday nights, I could listen to the

re-broadcast of Monday Night Football aired on a Tijuana television station after the game concluded in the U.S. Not knowing Spanish, I made it a habit to look up when the announcer sounded excited about something. On one occasion, I was carrying a model to the house when I spooked a baby skunk and was sprayed at point-blank range. I had to apologize for how my model *smelled* in class the next day.

3 In San Francisco, my beloved dog and I lived in a studio apartment with the bed in a corner flanked by fabric-covered flats and floor-to-ceiling shelves of books with bungee cords drawn across them for fear an earthquake might hit and books would come tumbling out. I (wisely) did not own a car there so traveling to do shows in other cities typically meant renting a car, loading up the dog and my belongings, and hitting the road. During one summer, I put 7,500 miles on a rental car in five weeks. When asked by the front desk clerk if I "went anywhere interesting," I handed him the keys and calmly replied "New Hampshire."

And I am not going to lie—I LOVED it. Every minute of it. Every one of those tiny spaces was my creative home and a dedicated design cave meant for that purpose only. It was a "maker space" before that term was even coined. It was a reminder of who I am and what I do. It legitimized me . . . to me. And it should legitimize you to you.

Many artists thrive in individual settings where they are content and perfectly happy as art introverts. For some (myself included), there is a certain bliss to being left alone in a studio setting with a full or partially full tank of inspiration and a rogue determination to claw-and-scratch something into existence that has not previously existed. For approximately half of the time, that is essentially the life of a designer. The "to do" list can be about as amorphous as a "to do" list has ever been: "figure out an idea for X" and "do sketches for Y." Inside of those loose parameters is a ton of room for a designer to simultaneously explore the limits of an idea about a project and plumb the depths of their own abilities. And, when it is going well, all that you create is brought to life in a very safe individual artistic space both literally and figuratively. You can have the music you want on with the beverage of your choice and create in that space to your heart's content. And the figurative space allows you some safety in the chaos of creation: "no one is around to judge these creations except me . . . at least not yet."

No matter how small, your studio should be your sanctuary. Particularly in this time of uncertainty about virtually all live performance artforms, your studio should be your space to explore your "why." The stoppage of work for almost all freelance creative artists and beyond ultimately means retreating to your studio to keep the flame burning. A pause to turn inward for inspiration rather than our normal outward collaboration. Your "studio" could be the back half of a kitchen table in a basement apartment but declaring that space your "studio" allows you the freedom to own your art and focus on defining what the next generation of storytelling might look like. In fact, you might think of both halves of that kitchen table in different ways: the front half feeds your body, and the back (studio) half feeds your curiosity and artistic soul. Dedicating a space to your own craft is to own a tiny real-estate holding on the vast theatre planet populated by artistic misfits like us. Own it. Stake your claim. Set your creative agenda for yourself and use that space as a laboratory for safe artistic exploration.

Time

When was the last time you caught yourself losing track of time entirely? Perhaps forgetting to eat or bathe or generally get into a "zone" from which your mind, your hands, and your whole psyche was in sync. Do you recall a moment or moments like that when the words just seemed to pour on to the page or the paint seems to just dance off the brush? Maybe you were just lost in some thoughts while washing the car or mowing the lawn. Basketball players who get hot on the court begin to see plays in slow motion and they choreograph moves and hit baskets almost effortlessly. They are in that zone for as long as it lasts. They feel the euphoria of riding that wave for as long as they can.

Hungarian psychologist Mihaly Csikszentmihalyi calls this concept "flow."[7] Once in flow, it can be the most exhilarating feeling in the world. You are in a bubble creating, adapting, and creating again. Your focus is heightened, and your tank of creative gas is bottomless. It is a wave that carries you and allows you to float on a sea of productivity. You are in the "flow channel".

Should something you are doing be too challenging, you fall out of that zone. Likewise, should it be too easy or boring, you fall out of the zone on the other side of the channel. Compare it to an ascending staircase: for each rise of difficulty, there is a run of completion within your capabilities and aspirations. Each step gets you higher and more addicted to the feeling of being in that zone.

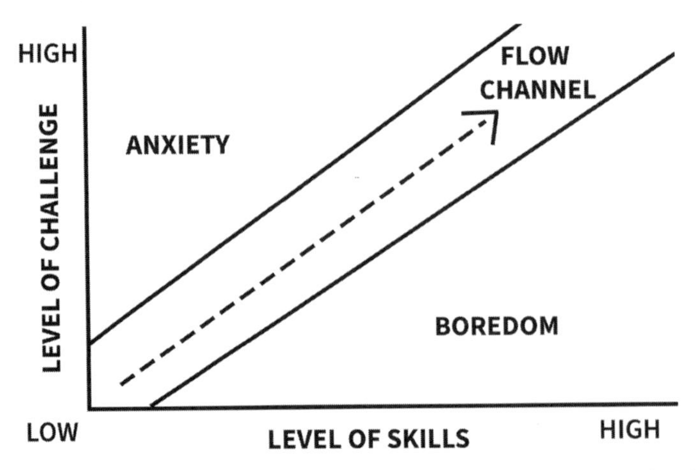

Figure 4.2 The "Flow Channel" Conceived of by Psychologist Mihaly Csikszentmihalyi. *Source: Marlies P Schijven.*

But there is absolutely no way to be in flow while "multi-tasking." As I saw in a meme once, Facebook, Twitter, Instagram, Snapchat, TikTok, etc. are all "weapons of mass **distraction**" when it comes to establishing a boundary of time for you and your work. Any artist worth their salt will tell you that there is no way to be creative while playing whack-a-mole with administrative tasks and distractions. Those distractions inherently disrupt flow, should flow even begin in the first place. You must give yourself time to craft, react, and to craft some more. Doesn't matter *what* you are creating; could be a chair or a pot or a stage set. Time must be on your side and belong to you. That time must be free of distractions that could mean interruptions in your flow and thought. That includes dedicated daydreaming and rabbit holes of research. It all adds up to your process. No one is saying that you must spend forty-eight hours at a stretch in flow and no one is advocating that you spend three days locked in a studio shed. But there is nothing selfish in stating to yourself and whomever else may need to hear it that the next three hours are about swimming out from the shore of your creative process and finding a wave to ride. If you're lucky, you may find one and it will be worth the journey from the safety of the shore.

The Design Digestive System

So, there you are with a copious amount of research in the form of books with post-it tabs on specific pages, some internet research you perhaps printed out, and perhaps some clippings brutally ripped from once-pure and intact magazines. You have spread them out on a table or on the floor and plopped yourself in the middle of that melee of visual musings. Now what? Something magical happens now, right? A conical whirl of inspiration floats over me and touches down like a tornado to stir up all this great research into one beautiful, assimilated, visual image that becomes the design . . . right? The brochure we have in our minds about being a designer clearly advertised that. Right? Even the last chapter of this book seemed to imply that the research was key. The rest of the process should be coasting down a hill of creativity in a derby car of pure emotion, bliss, and brilliant ideas with friends and colleagues on the fringes of the track cheering me in the form of social media "likes." I mean, right? That is how it works, correct?

Sadly, no. I wish that were the case. I wish we could each have a unicorn that farts glitter as well, but that's not a thing either.

The present moment in the process is more like a digestive system than a downhill derby race. This is the moment where you internalize all that great dramaturgical and visual research you have done to this point, ingest and digest it like a nomadic African wildebeest south of the Sahara, and force out (I'll spare those details) a somewhat formed block of something that may—or may not—resemble the beginnings of a design or an idea for a design. Apologies for the visual you may have in your mind at the moment, but my aim was a study of contrasts, I suppose. Nothing like comparing anything to excrement as a literary tool to drive a point home.

Avoiding the Self-edit

In my university course on creativity, I regularly do an exercise with students developed by J.P. Guilford in 1967 called the Alternative Uses Test.[8] In my adaptation, I leave off the word "test" and call it an exercise. After all, nothing increases a student's blood pressure more than the word "test" spoken aloud in a classroom. The exercise is a relatively simple one: students are prompted to have a pencil and paper and are given an insanely short amount of time (about two minutes) to come up with thirty uses for a random object. With the rules of the game understood, I share the object and start the countdown. The object can be virtually anything: a chair, a basket, a potato—anything. During those two minutes, some students furiously write while others stare at the object and write a use down every twenty-five seconds or so. Rarely, if ever, do participants actually achieve the required thirty uses for the object. A poll of the students afterward usually yields some typical results:

1 The most common use is always listed first. For example, if the object is a chair, "sit on it" and "stand on it" are the first to uses written on the page. That is an easy and obvious two uses.
2 While speed is a necessity, some students put down a shorthand answer that, when explained post-exercise, actually leads to a complex answer for that use.

Take that post-exercise reflection a step further and a profound truth emerges: we self-edit. *Constantly.* Like a program operating in the background on our device, the self-editing process is always on whether we are aware of it or not. The time constraint in the exercise is not meant increase student blood pressure (although it may) and is not a conceit meant to get us through the exercise and on to the lecture in double-time. The time constraint forces us to not self-edit our ideas. It forces us to stay a step ahead of the demons and doubters in our own minds that might cause us to *not* write down a use for the object. After all, the goal is a *multiplicity* of ideas and time is the limiter. Your self-editor in your mind might snap back: "That's a silly idea ..." only to be reprimanded by the non-editor in your brain reminding you of the rules: "Go for it. Put it down. It counts as one idea! Let's move on. You are running out of time!"

We humans have preconceptions and biases about our own abilities that consistently impair us from sharing our unique gifts with the world. Whether it be a classroom with eighty other students or a conference room with six other people, we have a tape-loop running an internal monologue which serves as a pretty good limiter to truly innovative ideas ... or at least the seedlings for one. You likely have heard these on a loop in your own head in response to a general query along the lines of "Does anyone have an idea/thought/response to this question?"

1 I have an idea for this, but I don't want to appear stupid in front of my peers if the idea has been (insert options here) made already/discussed already/proposed and failed already/etc.
2 I know Jack/Jill are the experts on this topic, so I'll hold back and give them space to say/not say what I think they are going to say. My expertise in this area is not as refined/valuable/insightful.
3 I proposed a solution to this in another class/company/meeting and it died on the vine/received ridicule/lost traction because Bob didn't like

it. I came away from that experience feeling terrible about myself/my idea/my future and generally mad at Bob. (there's always a Bob we could do without—am I right?)

4 I have a *great* idea for this challenge, but I don't want to show up my peers for fear they'll ostracize me in the classroom/conference room/breakroom. Best choice is to not "rock the boat," right? Slow and steady wins the race.

It is my solemn belief that we all have these germinations of ideas that get as close as the threshold of the open door but never pass through that opening to see the light of day. Think of it: if ideas were FedEx packages, consider leaving an "ah-ha" epiphany that can lead to a cure for cancer or a preliminary idea for ridding the oceans of toxins or any other potentially revolutionary thought on the front porch in a package that is never opened. Every day, countless ideas are left at the stoop and never opened because we have collectively decided that being vulnerable is the worst thing that can happen to someone. We view vulnerability as a flaw or secret shame we should never openly admit we possess. In an era when we have democratized speech and ideas and thoughts that we freely share online and that can travel across the world in a millisecond with the tap of a button, we have somehow conversely decided that we cannot risk a crazy idea with our peers in a vastly smaller setting. Why is that?

> The day before something is truly a breakthrough, it's a crazy idea.
>
> Peter Diamandis, Co-Founder of XPrize (quoting Burt Rutan)[9]

Your Inner Clown

My old summer-stock theatre collaborator and university colleague Kato Buss has a Tedx Talk that attempts to convey the power of vulnerability using a simple and yet elegant comparison: the clown.[10] As we all know, the clown is that one part of the circus act who embraces all of the self-deprecating fears that drive those inner monologues in our head and prevents us from speaking up and out in front of our peers. The clown not only welcomes but *invites* that kind of ridicule packaged in the context of a series of pratfalls and goofy mistakes in a quest to illicit laughter from adults and children alike. The clown is a Harlequin character representing pure vulnerability. Consider the courage that it takes to play the fool for an audience: what a virtue to possess the ability to play around with ideas and have no reservations in sharing them. As Kato describes, we all have a clown:

> What I know is that the clown—my clown, your clown, all of ours—stands there with this wonderful childlike imagination with empathy and vulnerability and looks at that fear (of failure), opens its eyes and its mouth and just . . . steps in.
>
> Present. In the moment. Imagine! Imagine if we lived like that.[11]

The child and the clown both have the strength and courage to be vulnerable. They possess an ability to stand both within and outside of themselves and balance what is and what is not working. The adult impulse is not to try for fear of failing. The child and the clown both know failure is just part of the journey toward success.

What is Working? . . . and What isn't?

> Well, one of the pictures I did in 1946, the one like a butcher's shop, came to me as an accident. I was attempting to make a bird alighting on a field . . . suddenly the lines that I'd drawn suggested something totally different, and out of this suggestion arose this picture. I had no intention to do this picture; I never thought of it in that way. It was like one continuous accident mounting on top of another.
>
> Francis Bacon[12]

The sketching-and-clawing phase in any artform is by no means easy. Consider an actor onstage: how do they know that a line is "working" or not? Following a lengthy rehearsal process in front of a director, the true test is in front of an audience. Do they react? Does it affect them? Does it elicit the response they seek?

In contrast, design is a much more of a solitary experience. In the months prior to when it is revealed onstage, a design occupies a corner of your studio table on a scale small enough to manipulate and private enough that no one has to see it until you are ready. In those moments, you must be of essentially two minds . . . and not go crazy balancing them both. Design requires you to hold two opposite truths in your head at once: you are simultaneously the artist and the *viewer* of that art. You must stand both inside and outside of yourself at once viewing your work by simultaneously knowing the genesis of it as an artist and knowing nothing at all about it in your role as a viewer.

Perhaps that notion sounds insane, but I would wager it is not at all a foreign concept to almost any artist of any flavor whether you are a writer, painter, or designer. Legendary designer Ming Cho Lee has been known to instruct young designers and students to "have a glass of wine, come back, and look at it (your design) again."[13] Looking past a potential issue with underage drinking, what is implicit in those instructions is the essential need to see a design with fresh eyes in order to properly answer the question almost every artist has muttered under his or her breath when seeing their work anew: "Is this working?" Is the art saying what you want it to say? If the set is another character, how does the character look, act, behave, speak, etc.? If the set is a sculpture, what emotions should it conjure in the viewer? Does it both say something and leave something for the audience or viewer to figure out on their own? Does it prompt a conversation on the car ride home which cuts to the heart of what the theatre production is meant to say to an audience? And in so doing, have we asked the audience to step outside of themselves as well? Have we prompted them to see a point-of-view that they had previously ignored or never even considered?

Answering "What If? . . ." with your Pencil

So back to the scenario painted in your mind at the beginning of this chapter: the "analogy of excrement," we'll call it. In that scenario, you are surrounded by the fruits of your labor in the form of your exhaustive research and . . . a blank page.

That blank page. How can something so unassuming and plain be such a difficult place to begin for any artist? So daunting, sometimes, that the first pencil stroke can feel like the most difficult one of all. I can recall buying an expensive piece of watercolor paper when I was a starving student and just fretting over marring that surface with anything. How could I risk ruining it when I couldn't risk having to buy another one? Whether it is the blank page or empty model box, know that the highest of high authorities in art and design have ALL been there.

With the aspirations and courage born from channeling your own inner clown, just . . . *draw*. Just begin thinking with your pencil on the page and noodle and doodle your way around. I personally find it helpful to pose wild ideas to myself with each one beginning with two words: What if . . .

1. "What if we had a this that was that way and a this that went this way . . ."
2. "What if I took this bit of research, blew it up, and reassembled the parts like this . . ."
3. "What if the whole set is (blue/metal/one wall/one door/40 feet high/etc)?

You are now immersed in the marvelous ideation phase of the design-thinking process. The we-could-try-this or we-could-try-that method of clawing and scratching out an idea. No rules apply to this phase. Upside down and backwards may very well lead to a glimpse of an environment that might work for the piece. Go for it. Get lost in the woods.

Just let your mind and your pencil flitter about on the page. Sounds completely insane, but channel the research, funnel it through your mind, send it down your arms to your fingers, and . . . play. Just *play*! Play around with wild ideas, curious musings, random threads, and streams of thought and make them visible in front of you. Instead of "dance like no one is watching" consider this an exercise of "sketch while no one is looking." What do you have to lose? Do not self-judge! Simply doodle. Draw faster than you can think. React. Even if only you know what it is you are drawing, that's all that matters. Your sketch may look like a cross between a schematic map for a subway system beneath the streets of Atlanta and an illustration of the capillary system of your favorite pet. Either way, it does **not** matter. What matters is that you channel an idea into a sketch as a means of trying the design jacket on the play. Does it fit? No? Noodle. Play some more.

And consider the medium in which you are working a liberating factor at play here. Set design is NOT a rigid medium necessitating a phalanx of engineers, architects, or structural code enforcers be added to the team. On stage, doors can float, and ceilings can fall. On stage, witches can rise from the floor and gods can descend from the heavens. On stage, trains can run in circles and cars can fly. The theatrical volume is a magical land where *anything* can happen, and *anyone* can do *anything*. It's a utopia where dreams co-exist with nightmares and stories need not be linear. Meant as a mantra and not a musical: Anything goes!

Realize ALL of that at THIS moment! Consider yourself a vessel of divine intervention and creative inspiration! It's time to seize those "ah-ha" epiphanies that come from putting the gas in the tank: the research, the study, the collaborative ideas with others, and even the if/then statements. This marks the end of the previous phase and the beginning of another. Your previous work is the muse for the work that follows. You have your brushes and paint about you. It's time to paint. You have your pencils and your paper about you. It's time to sketch. And I did not say that you should do anything but *sketch*.

1 I did not say get out your laptop and begin making walls and staircases in a 3D computer model.
2 I did not say to crack open a new CAD drawing and start putting digital lines on a digital page.
3 I did not say to open up Photoshop and begin manipulating photos of the room.

There is time for all that *later*. There will be time to use all the tricks and the tools that make your process more efficient and more polished. There will be time to refine the idea and form it into a sculpture that your colleagues and collaborators can understand. There will be a time to focus on everything from budget to automation and from staircase treads to cornice moldings.

That time is NOT now.

Now is solid lump of clay time. Now your hands are the tool fueled by your ideas and flowing from those ideas to your pencil. Think with the pencil! Shut down the inner voice that tells you "You can't draw." This is not about drawing. This is about clawing and scratching. This is about a dialogue and back-and-forth between your mind and your hand. That's it. Sounds simple. It's not. Sounds necessary. It is.

And if the epiphanies, ideas, and inspiration don't come? Stop. Have a glass of (blank—appropriate to your present age) and come back to the pile of research at another time. It will wait. It will wait for your creative courage to refuel and rebound. It will wait for that moment at the dinner table when, in a discussion completely unaffiliated with this show or this project, an idea pops into your head and a torrent of "what if's" come streaming forth. Kurt Vonnegut was known for leaving his own dinner parties and adjourning to a room to write because a fleeting idea struck him and capturing that thread at that time was more important than socializing and entertaining his own guests. In her talk on creativity, Elizabeth Gilbert, author of *Eat/Pray/Love* tells a story of American poet Ruth Stone who grew up on a farm in Virginia. Ruth would be working in the fields and feel a rumble that would shake the earth under her feet:

> She knew that she had only one thing to do at that point, and that was to—in her words—run like hell. And she would run like hell to the house. And she'd

be getting chased by this poem. And she had to get to a piece of paper and a pencil fast enough so that when it thundered through her, she could collect it and grab it on the page. And other times, she wouldn't be fast enough. She'd be running and running and running and she wouldn't get to the house and the poem would barrel through her. And she would miss it. And she said it would continue on across the landscape looking, as she put it, for another poet.[14]

Space, Time, and the Default Mode Network

Students, and even some design colleagues, have a backwards way of thinking about time. We tend to look at a set of deadlines and think about how they might fit in our overall scope of work. Every freelance designer not beholden to a company may, at any given time, have a patchwork quilt of projects to do with design deadlines associated with each one. Keeping all the clients happy and the balls in the air is a challenge, but so is affording yourself the time to reject more ideas than you accept. That takes time.

Basic human nature might lead us to believe that we put off starting a project until we *need* to focus on it and get it in by the deadline. Why do today what we can put off to tomorrow, right? After all, I've got other x, y, and z things to do today. As a high-school student, I recall being ridiculed by my sister for doing homework on a Friday night for assignments not due until Monday. I recall what drove me to such (perceived) insanity: the notion that the homework would be cloud hanging over my head the entire weekend if I did not just take care of it on a Friday night. Completing it on Friday night gave me the freedom to be as carefree as I wanted the entire weekend—including Sunday night. In that instance, the clarity of thought and freedom from obligation is what drove the early-over-late decision to complete a project or an assignment.

Design has another muse at play in the "start the project early rather than late" argument. Time affords you the opportunity to fail—and iterate—and ponder—and sculpt a shape. Delaying a start on a design only further compromises your process—and thereby your chances of any measure of success with it. A design deadline in March does not mean you start the clawing and scratching in late February. You may be able to get it done and feel your abilities and skills can allow you to "turn it around," but you shortchange the aspect of the designing that cannot be rushed: the "percolate" phase.

Commonly in reference to coffee, percolate was a favorite word of mine growing up. It essentially references the opposite of the "ah-ha epiphany" we think all artists have (and they often don't). To allow a concept time to percolate means that you're giving it time to simmer on the back burner of your brain.

There is a scientific aspect of brain science pioneered by Dr. Marcus Raichle called the Default Mode Network.[15] The concept quite simply points to the fact that our brains are actually quite active when we have no realization that they are at all. While sleeping and daydreaming, our brains are actually working on problems and challenges we placed at the front of our cerebral cortex perhaps days earlier. Ever come up with a solution in the morning shower to a problem that seemed so vexing the night before? Your brain was working on it—while you (technically) were not.

Time affords you the opportunity to become hyper-aware. Allow me to explain. Two possible scenarios could play out for the production of a play that opens in July, for example, for which you got the assignment in January:

1. You read the play in January well ahead of the design deadlines and discover that a number of the scenes take place in an old barn. For the next three months, you are hyper-aware every time you see a photo or pass an old barn on the highway. You take mental notes of the structure, shape, condition, etc. You take photos with your phone to put into your file for the piece. Your hyper-awareness—afforded by the simple luxury of *time*—allows you to research as you go.
2. You read the play in June just before the design deadline. You discover that a number of the scenes take place in an old barn. You do a mad dash to the library or skip that and see what comes up when you do an internet search of the word "barn." You are rushed. You are stressed. You don't make educated guesses or logical choices because company X wants drawings soon.

Honestly: why would you put yourself through the anguish of the second scenario? It just makes no sense. Read the play as soon as you receive it. Allow time to "percolate" on research and pay attention to barns along the way.

Time also affords possibilities for failure at *no* cost. And by failure, I really mean "experimentation" and "iteration," the lifeblood of any design process. The rejected ideas or "something's not right" thoughts about a design need time to be figured out and eventually resolved. Time allows for clawing and scratching to happen and for concepts to develop. The grasping, while difficult, needs time to grasp. To add a layer of stress to the blank-page phobia just add a tight deadline that will only serve to force you to "shoot from the hip" with half-baked ideas and no time to fully vet them with your creative team colleagues and fellow artists. The awkward Vonnegut party departures and Ruth Stone races to the poem on the page were all made possible because time *allowed* ideas to percolate for a while and inspiration to strike. Whether you call it the "back of your mind" or the default mode network, your brain needs *time* to do that work. Waiting to start a project until you think you "need to" does not help you . . . or anyone else working with you for that matter. It only shortens the amount of time your brain has to work on ideas in the background and around the edges of your psyche. Ideas need time to percolate. They cannot be summoned at will and based on impending deadlines.

So, *start early*. Read the play early and think about it for weeks if you have it! Pull on an idea thread and see if it unravels the whole thing: it just might create an entirely new awe-inspiring garment!

5

Modeling and Shaping an Object and an Idea

Chapter Outline

You are Your own Instrument

After the clawing and scratching comes the leap of faith to an extent. You have a rough sketch you think worthy enough to push forward and try-the-jacket-out on the play. Maybe it is a bit snug? Perhaps a bit too loose around the shoulders? Maybe the sleeves are a little short? But you know that there is something there, something you can't quite put your finger on, that seems to represent your labors to this point delving into research and discussing worlds with your collaborators. *Something.*

We are at a stage of the process that resembles the prototyping phase of the design thinking process. At some point, a mock-up of the design jacket must be tailored to see if you are on a pathway that resonates not just for you, but for the design team and director as well. "Quit aiming and fire!" If you are crafting a novel or a story or a poem, there must be some words on the page to edit and manipulate into a finished work. Here, you must sculpt an idea into a shape.

Most challenging about this phase is the perhaps the leap of faith required to believe that an idea is worth moving forward when you—and no one else—can know if it will work or not. That is completely the case. After all, you may later find that the journey down this particular path leads to a dead-end or an unworkable design idea. I know what that dead-end looks like! I have been there many times. So, it's safe to say that knowing what a bad design idea looks like may be just as important as knowing a good one when you are lucky enough to find it.

Filmmaker David Lynch was the subject of an interview once whereby he compared an idea to having bait on a hook. A good idea is just the first initial morsel on that hook that you hopefully use to attract ideas—to act as bait—for more ideas that further clarify and inform the larger idea. With enough attraction and enough ideas attracted to that original morsel idea, you may find yourself with a painting or a chair or a script or a set design. Believing in that first idea is the key to the entire process. You may end up with more ideas hooking onto that first idea bait only to find what forms is not at all the right approach. The conglomerate of the total idea stack is definitely a *larger* idea, but … not an approach that seems right for the play. And you will know that when you see it.

Think of it: Chuck Berry, Miles Davis, and Duke Ellington all performed thousands of times and for many millions of people in the process. But they each were the only ones on the planet who heard every performance they ever did. They heard every note of every concert. The same is true for the work you have created, the writing you have done, the noise in your head—you're the only person who has heard every bit of it. To me that means that you are your own instrument. Call it talent, call it instinct, call it intuition—whatever you want to call it, you know in your gut what you are capable of and what looks/sounds/feels right in the artistic medium you have chosen to pursue.

You may mutter to yourself: "this isn't quite right" or "something's missing." Your jacket mock-up may not fit. That's OK. The experience comes when you know when to wander back out to the beginning again and bait the hook with a new idea. Every artist worth their salt will tell you that they experience just as many if not more of these dead-end journeys as successes. Nothing comes easy. Nor should it, I suppose.

> A smooth sea never made a skilled sailor.
>
> Franklin D. Roosevelt[1]

Don't Tell Me, *Show* Me

In high school, I had a U.S. Government teacher named H. Jack Woods. On the first day of class, Professor Woods began by essentially reciting his qualifications for teaching government by listing items off of his own lengthy resume including multiple years serving in the Texas State Legislature beginning in 1959 and serving on multiple committees from Public Lands and Buildings to School Districts and Criminal Law. He concluded by simply announcing to us "I don't have to be here." On a dime, that changed the dynamic of the entire course for the rest of the semester. On a dime, the class changed from being a daily obligation to fulfill a requirement on our high school transcript to a profound sense that it was a privilege to be a bunch of teenagers with bad acne in a room with someone of that experience who did not have to but *wanted* to teach us. At that moment, the class was less about the grade or the transcript notation and more about the learning and the education of young minds. Not surprisingly, the class was not your typical government class by any means. We did briefly cover the three branches of government and the role of circuit courts in the judicial system. But H. Jack spent much of the time professing the importance of being an informed citizen who goes into a voting booth having done their civic duty of studying the issues in advance. We were to be prepared to vote on a bill or a candidate based on what H. Jack called "gnosis"—Greek meaning knowledge or awareness. There is not a single time I don't enter a voting booth without thinking of him. My (informed) vote is as much a duty to him and what he taught as it is to my country.

Like any Texan, H. Jack had a number of sayings he liked, that often seemed oddly quirky and confusing to teenagers assembled in his classroom, in a language that mixed complex legalese and judicial theories were phrases like "(the issue) is like a pancake, it's only got two sides." One saying in particular has stuck with me all these years: "The proof of the pudding is in the eating." At first, I was mystified by the phrase and had no idea why classroom conversation had shifted from pancakes to pudding. Ask my own students today and they will tell you that I often say it to them when discussing design. Plainly put, what H. Jack meant was that we can have theories about concepts and ideas, but something can only be truly judged and evaluated when it is put into practice. We are back into "quit aiming and fire" territory here. When applied to design, the "proof of the pudding" is that iterative process of showing ourselves—and our collaborators—visual ideas we manifested in our heads out in the open for all to see. Every design student who has ever lived has come into class on the day an assignment is due, shared perhaps a crude iteration of an idea, and then attempted to talk their way through an often-meandering explanation in an attempt to embellish what simply is not there to see. To show precious little in class while simultaneously painting a visual picture in words just does not cut it in the design world. Much like this very text, there must be words on the page for an editor to have any chance of crafting it into something worth printing. There must be something to show your collaborators and some meaningful progress displayed since the last time you shared valuable time together around a table discussing a production. For our craft, the "proof of the pudding is in the eating" is a more abstract way of saying "don't tell me, *show* me!" Our design language is entirely visual. Always default to the visuals. Don't tell me, *show* me.

The *Saint Joan* Saga

In 2009, I was tasked with designing an epic *Saint Joan* at the Repertory Theatre of St. Louis directed by Paul Mason Barnes. For me, the opportunity represented the culmination of a couple of chapters in my journey from being a student designer to being called a "professional". Twenty years earlier, in the spring of 1989, I was a high school senior and a recent victim of the theatre bug. A recruiter from a university in St. Louis was visiting and invited me to visit campus and see what a college experience at Webster University might look like for me. I made the journey and spent a day shadowing current students, attending classes, and generally becoming excited about the whole idea of a place where theatre wasn't just a high school extracurricular activity, but THE thing students studied and did and breathed 24/7. The night before departing for home, I was told that I should see a production of *Saint Joan* being put on by the Repertory Theatre of St. Louis, It was an opportunity to see a real professional production crafted by designers and actors and directors who were doing what I could only dream of doing at the time. I was told that I should see it, but that no tickets were available so I should sneak onto the catwalks suspended above the stage and watch it with a bird's eye view. I was enraptured by what I saw. The set, the lights, the costumes: everything was top notch.

Fast-forward twenty years to my young designer clawing and scratching days and I get a call by the artistic director of the same company to design the exact same play on the exact same stage. My initial response was "but you just did that play" to which he responded, "that was twenty years ago, Rob."

Having seen the 1989 production, I sensed the height of the high bar placed before me. I had to honor that production while collaborating on a new one for a new audience. It is fair to say that I was going to take this design seriously. I was going to do all my homework, explore all the avenues that the research offered, and not let my seventeen-year-old self down in the process. There might be another prospective student in the catwalks watching a production of this epic play that I designed, and I was not going to let him or her down. That was my goal. Having placed enough pressure on myself to warrant therapy a few times over, it was time to claw and scratch.

I began responding to the research that the director and I both loved. A lot of gothic archways amidst the ruins of an old Celtic church weathered by the sun and mist and the winds of time. A "crucible of space" was what he requested—a nod to what should have been a liberating idea to a designer: just create a stage that works for all five acts and multiple scenes. No need to "flesh out" every detail as long as we give the audience some sense of where we are in the play.

So, I went to work attempting to do just that. My early sketches allowed for seemingly grand gestures with tracking walls of Gothic tracery set against a vast expanse of color that could define everything from a sky to a wall of fire as needed (see plate 12).

But ... something "wasn't quite right." I admitted it to myself, and my director (thoughtfully) reiterated it to me as well. Sketch after sketch of this design just did not seem to provide the—let's say—visual gravitas that this epic tale demanded. It was just ineffective and lacked the grandeur required for an epic tale. No level of embellishment in the computer through layers of color or applications of shadow brought it to the promised land where we could continue moving forward knowing that we had found our "crucible of space" for the play. It was a terrifying feeling. You know that you are not where you should be for a concept, but you also have no idea which way to go either. Like being at an intersection with dozens of "this way" and "that way" signs out of an old Bugs Bunny cartoon—you just feel lost.

But notice that I have avoided the word "failure" to describe these meandering missions that led to an empty stream: that's because they are ***not***! There is intrinsic value in the experimentation in your studio laboratory just as there is in a scientific lab of any kind. Play-Doh, x-rays, and Velcro were all *accidental* discoveries. Accidental discoveries abound in these uncertain circumstances, and you can be assured that every success necessitated multiple iterations and experiments (not failures) to get there. If scientists can call making controlled mistakes "experiments", then why can't you? Your studio is your laboratory minus the high-tech equipment and potential hazards related to chemicals (depending on the studio).

> I have not failed. I've just found 10,000 ways that won't work.
>
> Thomas Edison[2]

Speaking as the recipient of a pair of non-scientific college degrees and based on absolutely zero scientific facts, I remain convinced that we all SEE in different ways. A design professor of mine could loosely draw-up a 2D plan view of a set with doors and windows and archways and stairs, turn to those of us in the class and ask "see that? . . . that'll work as a plan for play X!" Hours later, I was still struggling with answering the "see that" part of the question. In truth, I could not see it at all. How does he know what "that" looks like and, if you get that far, how do you know that it'll work for play X anyway? And back up a step more: who said we needed walls at all? The point is: he saw it, but I (and others) simply did not. And we did not . . . for about three years. I tried over and over to think in plan view and elevate the plan view in my mind, but it only frustrated and mystified me, and the imposter syndrome would return. I convinced myself that I was not gifted with the ability to see a design that way.

By some divine act of pity or grace (I'm still not quite sure) that professor took a sabbatical in my fourth year of college and two incredibly influential design and life mentors entered Stage Left to replace him for eight weeks each: Carolyn Ross and Michael Ganio. It was from them that I learned that I could have another approach. Sounds simple, but at that age, I thought the plan-to-elevation method of seeing a design was the only one out there . . . and I was a failure at it. Carolyn and Michael each had a more-sculptural style of working on a design that prompted a designer to ask: if I am going to *end up* in 3D, perhaps I should start in 3D? The whole approach was thrilling to me! Start with objects made from non-precious bits of cardstock and matte board. A snip-snip there and a slice or a fold there, place it in the model volume, judge the result, remove it, modify it, and begin again. It was such a different (not better) process! It was an entirely new way to SEE a design. Eureka! I may have a future in this crazy business after all.

So—back to the sordid self-dubbed *Tale of the Terrible Tracery*: It was, of course, time to try a new approach and the "ah-ha" moment came when I decided to shift mediums. I grabbed some cardstock and began snipping with little hope of making something. At this point, I would have honestly been happy to make *anything*. A crude nativity scene would be nice. Just . . . something. Referencing the research yet again, I realized that I desperately wanted and could not achieve the sense of awe that any of us feel when we enter a historic church. It is the height that plays to our sense of spiritual wonder. Of course, that height is baked into the plans of any church. The use of height is intentional and gives us a sense of a higher power above us and, by comparison, we are but tiny subjects to that higher power. Perhaps you have felt that way walking into a church? The prescribed reaction is, and always has been, awe. But how to achieve that in a theatre that is only about twenty-four feet tall? That restriction felt like a straitjacket. So, I fumbled around.

The negative space off-cut from a floor shape was sitting next to the model. Mumbling to myself, I thought—if only I could have THIS kind of height in the room planting the two legs of a pointed Gothic arch into the model. Almost as if on cue, the top portion of the arch folded over like a wet noodle drooping under the weight of its own shape curving downstage and over the audience itself.

Ah-ha! The clawing and scratching had finally paid off! Whether or not I could pay off my student loans was another matter, but this is it! This is . . . *something?!* And thus, began the process. The downhill derby race had

Figure 5.1 Paper Model Design for *Saint Joan* at the Repertory Theatre of St. Louis. *Source: photo/design by author.*

begun. All of the other decisions that followed seemed minor by comparison and tended to naturally fall into place. Finally! The proper hook was baited now.

The Model: It's not Jewelry. Don't Fall in Love

As you have likely experienced in your own work, the hardest part of the process was the not knowing. We ask that an audience enter a space to see a story and take a risk of not knowing, but here, in our own craft, that not knowing can be terrifying. It is in those moments that the internal monologue of "who do you think you are?" or "are you good enough for this?" starts on a replay inside your head. Perhaps little-by-little at first, but seemingly building and feeding off the struggle. Don't let it! You are the scientist in a lab. Experimentation is necessary.

In the documentary cited earlier, Gehry gives a tour of his studios and shares examples of what are ostensibly multiple iterations of multiple models all representing a step in the process of a building becoming a building. From a sketch to fruition. Some models are crafted of plastic, others metal, some cardboard, or just a combination of sticks and wood-glue. He was certain to point out they all were meant to represent a stage in development of the exact *same* building. One could see similarities, but why so many and why formed and crafted out of so many different materials? Gehry simply replied "it keeps me real."[3] It keeps me real. A simple phrase to say that he checks himself—as all designers do—when they rehearse the future. It is a way of saying that this object is not the objective. Gehry elaborated those multiple iterations representing steps along the way kept him focused on the real building. Otherwise, the model might "become jewelry" and he never wanted that to happen.[4]

The exchange represents a fundamental ideal in this iterative experimentation we call designing. Unlike Gehry, many of us who call ourselves freelance designers do not have fleets of assistants working in various materials in a massive shop tackling multiple projects at one time. Maybe you do, but then I doubt you would be reading this book for my advice. I should be soliciting yours! Not all that different from our siblings in the architecture realm, we spend long hours and many nights crafting and refining a tiny scale sculpture of a model. The mediums and materials change, but the solitude that comes with working on a model under some tiny lights in a studio can be quite intoxicating. Talk about flow! Hours can go by and it may feel like ten minutes. You might forget to eat, or you might attempt to craft one more tiny quarter-inch-scale chair, table, or floor lamp before you "go to bed" only to find out that morning is around the corner. You've been there. The feeling is the same in any medium. You're on a roll. Why interrupt it with life, right?

But the lesson of "keeping it real" must remain no matter the cost to the (let's face it) "jewelry" you have laboriously created. It is not a Fabergé egg. You must remind yourself, as Gehry did, that the focus should always be on the real thing—the *real* design—the eventual "full-scale model." That is and should always be the focus. You must be willing to sacrifice attachment to the design as an object for that ideal.

In graduate school, I was summoned to my design professor's office and told that he had a message for me related to my financial aid. Somewhat anxious, I booked the appointment and met with him. I had a scholarship that I desperately needed to afford graduate school paid for by SeaWorld and, according to my professor, they "wanted something for their money." I was instructed to contact them, arrange an appointment, and go to SeaWorld through the employee entrance. I fully assumed that I would be issued a uniform, a pair of rubber boots and told to get to work cleaning buckets, painting tanks, or scraping bird poop off of multiple surfaces I could not yet imagine.

To my surprise (and relief), I was put to work designing for them. I designed a non-animal X-Games style obstacle course on an island in Mission Bay and spent time in that tiny shed/studio in the backyard (a bit more wary of skunks now) crafting a soldered brass scaffolded model in quarter-inch scale. It was like a pinball game turned vertically with all kinds of levels and whirligigs. When I brought it into the offices to share it with members of the team, I was given input that offered me insights on what was and was not possible: "the logo can't be there" and "the jump from there-to-there is too tall" (see plate 13).

And then it happened: I began to rip portions of the model apart on the spot in a way that better reflected the recommendations they offered me. The team members were horrified. "What are you doing?" they asked, "You're *ruining* it!" To them, the model *was* jewelry. As I explained to them, the model is a tool to get us to the real thing. Much better to make mistakes in this phase than with real steel with contractors watching and waiting. *Now* is the time to make mistakes. Not later. As an old boss of mine used to say: "It's easier to fix with an eraser than a crowbar."

Modeling as Prototyping

The model is essentially the prototype for what may become a larger ... something. What I found profound about exploring the world of design thinking and human-centered design after spending years in the theatre were the remarkable similarities. Phase four of the five-step process of design thinking is prototyping, but what that means in ten different disciplines could mean ten different things. Important to note here that "prototyping" may be perceived as isolated to crafting an actual object, but a prototype can be so many different things as well.

1. Architects may indeed build a model prototype but crafting the experience for a client *inside* that building is as important (and as expected) today as it has ever been by clients. "I want to walk inside it" is now a viable option for a client.
2. In a book called *Creative Confidence*, IDEO shares examples of constructing an entire pharmacy out of foamcore to prototype the experience of getting a prescription start-to-finish for a typical customer.[5]
3. An app can be prototyped as a flow-chart that illustrates possible moves and choices like those in a chess game. Multiple landing pages can mean exponential possibilities for the app user. A simple (even paper) prototype can help identify these pathways for an app user.
4. Consider the worlds one inhabits at Universal Studios or Disneyland: those are experiences where you drop a patron inside of a designed world. The line between audience and actor is completely gone. Those experiences must be prototyped and tested before they are steel and fiberglass—right down to the lines of a queue on the way into the experience.

As with the *Saint Joan* model, my struggles in the ideation "what if" phase led me to essentially skip ahead to the prototyping phase of the process, but it was more than that in my opinion. What I was trying to do was a 3D *sketch*. To bust myself out of the artistic rut I was in creating less-than-satisfying designs for a piece that demanded a larger-than-life approach, I just started playing with paper and experimenting with forms. I embraced the "what if," but with cardstock and tape rather than pencils and tracing paper.

And remember that we did this all the time when we were children. Folding paper airplanes and giving them a launch off of the staircase joyous at the glide they had or the distance that each one traveled based on different tweaks to the overall design. A thinner look here or maybe a wider wing there yielded different results. As kids, we were constantly iterating, testing, and reiterating to get a different result. Sledding down a snowy hill demanded multiple tries using various types of sleds and other objects that might be loosely called sleds. As a kid growing up in the South, we did not own sleds nor could we buy them, but realtor signs made great "sleds." After those tests for speed and viability, next comes the inevitable multiple occupants version of a sled. Next thing you know, you are become a pile of human pinballs careening down a frozen hill at a high rate of speed.

So, don't skip this part! As described before, time can be a factor that causes you to skip steps on the way to completion. I've heard designers say, "I didn't have time to craft a model," and they are essentially saying they didn't have time to test the ideas to see if they work. That may be fine for a chair you are building for yourself or a circuit you're wiring, but the creative team snowball of artists and individuals invested in YOUR ideas and design only gets bigger from here. A shoot-from-the-hip style may work in the Wild West, but a designer who skips steps is making a series of errors and planting seeds for a series of mistakes along the way that crop up when you don't need them. Make mistakes late enough in a process and it means a shop is waiting on you for longer than they have time to wait or working diligently to fix something that *should* have been something you fixed with an eraser—and didn't. The usual mental crutch in these instances is that our perceived or real talent will carry us through and that our "shoot-from-the-hip" guesstimate that could have been slightly more accurate and less about guesswork isn't because we did not take the time needed to do the work. It is that simple.

> Design is 95% work and 5% talent.
>
> Unknown

Let's review the opposite extremes we are faced with as designers. Choose neither.

1. One extreme: do not do the model.
2. The opposite extreme: the model is precious "jewelry."

Spend just enough time on it to convey an idea (and get some sleep when you can). The rest will—and did—follow with the *Saint Joan* design (see plate 14).

In the end, we ended up with an appropriately epic design for an epic play about an epic woman warrior for the ages. Laid flat, the arch was 46 feet long from point to legs and had to be built upside-down by the talented artists/structural engineers in the shop. A repeating pattern of applique to the arch was devised to bend with the arch itself thanks to the contributions of the scenic artists who crafted it. It was, in the end, really *something*. I just had to live with the not knowing. Audiences did not see the angst and uncertainty of the journey. They only witness the end of the process.

> No artist is pleased. [There is] no satisfaction whatever at any time. There is only a queer divine dissatisfaction, a blessed unrest that keeps us marching and makes us more alive than the others
>
> Martha Graham[6]

6

Creative Swings, Career Fields, and Collaboration

Chapter Outline

Collaboration is Key

In the opinion of many in the business world, the days of the "rock star CEO" in the mold of Bill Gates and Steve Jobs are essentially over. To quote a publication by the Conference Board entitled *Go Where There Be Dragons: Leadership Essentials for 2020 and Beyond*:

> The CEO as Rock Star is dead. Leaders will need to be more collaborative and better listeners. Smart leaders won't do it alone—they will create great teams where group expertise matters more than individual savvy.[1]

With so much focus on empathy as the key to innovation, companies now have divisions of individuals that guide the organization using DESIGN processes. Building on ideas is the only path forward for companies. Collaboration and creativity are key. Creating environments where crazy questions can be asked, and "stupid" ideas proposed, allows companies to "rehearse the future."

As a theatre designer, we *rely* on creative interactions with others. You live a life of moments when you stop yourself and realize that what you can create with others is so much more than what you alone can create. You've perhaps felt the charge of an opening night that "fired on all cylinders" with your artistic collaborators and felt the sting of disappointment when it did not. You are the troubadour that Robert Edmond Jones speaks of, and your band of "poets and dreamers" are your theatrical family who join you in the ranks to create something—sometimes ANYthing—together and with each other. If you think back, you have lived moments when collaborative victories remain in your memory whether they involve drama or not. It may have been choir, marching band, or organized sports, but you've *lived* it. And, once experienced, the draw to return to it is strong. It is an adrenalin high that, once experienced, demands a repeat performance.

Collaboration is not an exclusively human endeavor. A visit to the zoo will produce a variety of examples of animals and insects working together towards a common goal. From bees and ants to monkeys and elephants, we can witness animals collaborating, protecting each other, foraging for food together, etc. The mourning doves outside my window right now always travel in pairs.

But I contend that humans are perhaps the only ones to actively create things together *beyond* our basic human animal needs. Being human means that we possess great powers to visualize what is not there and use our creativity to craft it into a reality ... sometimes with a lot of kicking and screaming. As humans, we possess an ability to collaborate on artistic works together in ways that are constantly adapting to advancements and technologies as well as manifesting themselves in new and interesting ways. From toasters to laptops to spacecrafts, we have consistently conceived of new ideas and new ways of collaborating to solve life's great mysteries and probe territories to explore that—we know—have an equal parts danger and possibility. We did—and continue to do—that.

I would also contend that we, as humans, actually NEED these types of interactions that allow us to leverage our ideas and build upon them with others. With every NASA rover that lands safely on Mars, we see that Mars rover as a symbol of the collective efforts of thousands of scientists, technicians, and explorers ... driving around on Mars in this one symbolic craft there to explore what man has never explored before. I BELIEVE to my core that THAT act is just as collaborative and creative as the finest opera at La Scala or the biggest hit musical on Broadway.

Looking back to Zefferelli's air vibrations, it is wise to note that those ideas do not see the light of day in our theatrical reality without the collaborative spirits of the collected artists in the room. Your design stays in the (dreaded) "non-realized" stage without the people who take your idea and run with it. A designer should never think they are a sole genius.

The Myth of The Sole Genius

Theatre is a *craft*—a marvelous collaborative craft with a family of friends and fellow artists who want to make magic with you. They want to help you achieve the vision you set out to create in the design. And it is always, always, wise to NEVER forget that, as a designer, that is a *privilege*—and *not* a right granted you. People have been gracious enough to believe in you. They have been selfless enough to go "all in" on an idea you had in your "mind's eye." They are willing to have you prove to them—and to yourself I might add—that your ideas are worth the time and effort and sweat to see them manifested in full-scale and in three-dimensions.

Designers may cite the simple fact that theatre artisans are paid for their work, but are they honestly paid that much when compared to other fields? They are there in that room with you and developing a world YOU dreamed up because they love the craft in the same way you do. They want to give themselves up for the greater good of the company of artists they represent. They love the collaboration in the same way you do. And—at their core—they want to see their work onstage, combined with the work of their artistic colleagues, making a silent beautiful and collective statement to an audience of fellow human beings who want to experience it.

My undergraduate schooling essentially took place in the basement of a theatre.

The Sargent Conservatory of Theatre Arts at Webster University holds a reputation in the theatre world as an undergraduate training program for wide-eyed theatre nerds like me who often defy the lofty aspirations that their parents had for them in exchange for a "follow your bliss" academic and vocational path in the exciting and perceived-as-glamorous world of the theatre. The forty-five or so undergraduate students in the design and technical areas were a panoply of different races and ethnicities with half-baked ideas about who we wanted to be in the "real world" beyond the confines of the campus. We clung to our idealized notions about a life in entertainment like a Titanic survivor clinging to a life raft. We were trainees for a battlefield of some kind—a battle against societal norms and conventions, perhaps. I cannot say that any of us were particularly sure of what we were studying or actually how we might apply it to the mystical "real life" we kept hearing about, but we were young and full of creative bravado. Late at night on a paint crew and feeling a bit punchy, we would hold our paintbrushes in the air and, channeling *Braveheart*, proclaim (to any idiot who bothered to listen to us): "You can take our brushes, but you can never take . . . our *freedom*!"

We began our late teens and twenties like a rag-tag bunch of art types seeking to prove something to our high school classmates who went off to study business or economics. To us, they were lemmings who had sold their soul when compared to our training towards somehow (we really were not quite sure) realizing a life of independence strapped to a free-wheeling spirit. We took big swings at the world in our own way through our untraditional design ideas and just as unconventional relationships with our peers. As often happens in college, late-nighters led to all-nighters. Working on fumes, ideas for possibilities and potentialities seemed more abundant, for some reason. The lines became blurred and the reservations about trying out ideas seemed to wane.

It was not at all uncommon to be conducting classes in the studios and facilities beneath the theatre itself and have sweaty actors launching themselves down the vom ramp exiting right into the hallways adjacent to those studios in full costume as if they've just entered modern life via some kind of portal connected to another era. The first few times this happened to me walking down a hallway, it was shocking. After a while, it just became part of a bizarre life. Theatre practitioners on the stage above and students studying to *be* like them in the basement below was just what was considered "normal" day-to-day faux reality. You'd pass a production assistant having a conversation about the next scene shift with an actor dressed in full battle garb wearing chain mail and carrying a sword next to some metal filing cabinets and a callboard displaying newspaper clippings and audition notices. All "normal." Upstairs was the laboratory for drama experiments and downstairs was teeming with support staff and chemicals being primed for the next (unintentional or intentional) explosion. From the get-go, the experience changed our preconceived venue for "work" from a stuffy metro office with shiny metallic ceiling fixtures and bottled water in a mini-fridge to a cavernous backstage area with thousand-pound scenic pieces floating overhead connected to a mini subway-system of underground tunnels and dressing rooms populated by everyone from orchestra musicians dressed in full formal wear to a stagehand wearing a faded black *Metallica '99 Tour* t-shirt. In that environment, one gets a sense that this business is different from the others.

By day, the hallways and classrooms of the basement were full of students following the instructions of faculty in all areas of theatrical training from dance to drama to design. Our design professor smoked during class. He drank Diet Coke out of one can and used another identical can for his cigarette ashes. In one instance, he drank the wrong one. It wasn't pretty. All the while, he made a point of repeatedly assigning us projects that prompted us to copy the work of the masters: a rendering project done in the style of Monet, or a portrait project done in the style of Rembrandt or Vermeer. The shackles were on us artistically—or so we thought. While applying gouache to an expensive piece of watercolor paper each of us could hardly afford, one of us had the courage to ask "Why do you make us do it this way? This isn't designing, this is copying." He took a drag from his cigarette and calmly replied: "Because you never truly know how great these artists are until you try to paint like them. And, with these limitations, when you get out of here, each of you will just *explode* with creativity."[2] Regardless of whether he made that up on the spot or was intentionally plotting this all along, it did give us some relief that we were in the position we felt we were in—that we were correct in feeling hemmed in and forced to run artistic drills rather than explore our own lofty design ideas and mental musings.

We were indeed in a bottle, and he was the cap.

The notion, however, stayed with many of us. It prompted us to have the courage to reframe and redefine ourselves once we obtained the diploma and walked across the stage. It made us realize that our twenties and thirties are about taking the greatest risks of our lives when the stakes are bigger, and our obligations are smaller. Youth is a feature and not a bug. What you don't know makes you blissfully unaware of what you don't know. But it also means you are completely unaware of the risks and potential pitfalls along the way that often turn away older and "wiser" adults who choose not to traverse that path or blaze a new trail. When you are a young professional, you essentially have no reputation to risk so risk away!

The sense of being capped or contained only to shoot forth from the post-graduation cannon was so liberating! It meant we could simultaneously incorporate our training and basic skills while plotting a path for ourselves that was unique to us in a way that was equal parts empowering and terrifying. It went against an unspoken but perhaps common understanding that you begin your college years pursuing that which is a "safe" career choice. With few responsibilities and fewer worries, why bother? Even the idea of a career *path* implies that we should be following some kind of predetermined career map in our life without access to . . . the map. How can we know the unknowable path? How do we know that it is right for *us*? At best, we have minimal guidance. No one told us where it begins, it's dark, and light sources are unavailable. Sometimes there are snakes and arrows that shoot out of cave walls along the way. Good luck! Carry on!

The Path vs the Field

When I lived in Denver, I was walking my dog Savannah one cold autumn morning in the only patch of grassy area in my largely urban neighborhood at the time: the parking lot for Coors Field where the Colorado Rockies play baseball. As it was almost every morning, my objective and the objective of countless dog owners like myself was to get the dog (and myself I suppose) some exercise, have her do her business, and get back into the warmth of the indoors. As with anything in life, the objective dictates the path—we are here to do something, let's get it done, follow the path, and get to our destination.

But this particular chilly morning was a little different: along the way, I found a dollar bill, then another, then a five-dollar bill, then a few more dollar bills, another five, etc. One by one, I was finding money not by looking ahead up the path, but all around me in the weeds and brush that lined the sides of the parking lot. For every look down and to the sides, I was struck by another bit of money just mysteriously lying there. In each instance, I stopped to pick it up only to catch another dollar bill out of the corner of my eye. As it turns out, a parking attendant's money box had blown open the night before scattering money everywhere.

I believe the story is a parable for a larger lesson to be learned and a metaphor for a way to look at a life journey as a creative: it can be deceptively easy to ignore the *field* if you are too focused on the *path*. To those that may have been watching me stopping to bend over and pick up bits of green paper on my dog walk that morning in Denver, they might surmise that I had lost my focus on the path that I had set for myself when I left the apartment leash-in-hand that morning. I was distracted by other things that left me exploring the merits of the field around me rather than focusing on the path ahead. Seems ridiculous, but there is a stigma placed on people who explore the fields, distractions, and diversions that always crop up around our own life path. There is a label placed on those individuals: "they lack focus" to do the work necessary to be the next great (blank). But they overlook that, most often, the "great ones" had their own seemingly unfocused forays as they danced across disciplines and found ways to innovate their own techniques and that is exactly what makes them the great (blank) they would eventually become.

All too often, we are tempted into believing that if we properly follow and execute path X then Y will inevitably follow. Achieving our dream in life is about performing a series of knob turns on a safe in precisely the correct order and pattern. Execute those steps and you'll be rewarded as the next great innovator or prodigy in the mold of those who came before. Should we wish to be a great hockey player, for example, we simply need to do exactly what "the Great One" Wayne Gretzky did to the letter from his childhood playing days onward. The all-time great Hall of Fame NFL receiver Jerry Rice used to lie in bed as a child in a pitch-dark room and throw a football in the air above himself in an attempt to catch it without being able to see it at all as it fell back down. Parents reading this might feel inclined to believe that having their child do the same drill will result in the same outcome. While great at what they did, Gretzky and Rice embraced the *field* along the journey of their life paths. Gretzky could not wait to drop his hockey stick and pads for a baseball hat and glove because he loved the awareness and strategy required for that game. Jerry Rice did not play football until his sophomore year of high school when a coach noticed that he could run fast. Both transformational athletes embraced the field around them, which allowed them to glean lessons and skills from other sports and passions. They were not following a formula. They were creating their own.

Following someone else's predetermined path for you is … following someone else's predetermined path. It is not yours. And why did I use the word "path" at all. Should we instead think of it as a field? Is that a more liberating turn of phrase for the journey? Myself and my classmates all left college wiser for the experience, but like most no surer at all of what would come next.

I would argue, that's exactly the way it should be.

> In an age where there is much talk about "being yourself" I reserve to myself the right to forget about being myself, since in any case there is very little chance of my being anybody else. Rather it seems to me that when one is too intent on "being himself" he runs the risk of impersonating a shadow.
>
> Thomas Merton[3]

Ask yourself this question about your own choice of study: do you love the training *and* the game? Seems easy to love the latter and much more difficult to love the former. For an athlete, there is a thrill during the game with the crowd cheering in a concoction of anxiety and expectation mixed with the pressure of the moment. Rewind to training camp amidst twice daily practices and mixed with some oppressive heat and the training really pales by comparison. But the greats love both in equal measure driven by two different prompts: the game is achievement in the external world while the training is internal achievement. The drive to train or, in the case of an artist, to hone your craft in the relative safety and isolation of one's own studio is spurred on by a willingness to experiment with the talents you have and innovate something new out of them. Trying these ideas out on an audience is the artistic equivalent of the thrill of the game for the athlete. Achieving some level of mastery of the basics (drawing, painting, model-building) allows for some freedom to try something new with those tools and in a way perhaps no one has seen before.

> "What can I make with this if I use the reverse side of the paper instead of the 'right' side?"
>
> "What happens if I do this drawing upside-down?"
>
> "What happens if I cut a piece of paper that clearly will not fit in the model and . . ."

All great creators from artists to athletes have sought to challenge themselves in order to satisfy their internal desires coupled with the external rewards. In the middle exists a marvelous balance between freedom and control. Between achievement and potential failure on the way to trying or doing or displaying something that no one has ever seen before. To those on the outside, it may seem an obsessive-compulsive disorder, but the goal is to get in the flow channel and ride the wave for as long as it will carry you. That's the addiction.

Professor Ellen Winner at Boston College has developed a theory as it relates to prodigies in any area or discipline. A prodigy in a specific area, she surmises, has a quality achieved by a balance of an obsession to learn in a domain and an ability to learn and gain ability quickly. The combination is called a "rage to master":

> It's an intense and obsessive interest, an ability to focus sharply, experiencing a state of flow when learning in their domain—optimal states in which they focus intently and lose sense of the outside world.[4]

For some, the process is more about mental survival than a desire to create. In an interview with photographer Norman Seeff, musician and producer will.i.am compares his mental capacity to a cup. He admits that he is constantly receiving stimuli in the form of lyrics, music, and song structures and, without some kind—any kind—of creative outlet, he risks breaking the cup and breaking himself. Essentially, he risks driving himself mad. These musings and manifestations of ideas *must* go somewhere or his cup—and perhaps your cup—will break. The outlet may be different, but we must strive to cherish moments when we have too many ideas for our own head to handle.

Don't Fit In. Don't Try to Fit In

Arts entertainment is, let's face it, a magnet for millions of misfits who do not fit into the buckets society has set up for the rest of us. I do not mean misfit in a derogatory sense. Quite the contrary. I mean misfit in the literal sense as in one who simply does not fit into any other category. The Merriam-Webster definition for "misfit" is "something that does not fit or that fits badly."[5]

And why *shouldn't* we embrace the difference rather than attempt to adapt and conform? For years, I've told my own students that "in a sea of suits, I hope they are the yellow bloomers." There is power in the non-conformist individual. In a world where we are supposed to "fit in" why do we assume that we need to do so in the first place?

I teach a class on creativity and find the first class to be the most important of the entire semester. It sets the tone for all the members of that particular boat on the journey. Highlighted by a series of examples, I run through the rather unconventional expectations for the course. For example, we think questions are more important than answers and finding yourself "in the woods" of a problem often leads to a more interesting and innovative answer to a question or challenge than if the pieces are all handed to you in a traditional teach-and-regurgitate facts-based course. We call that being "on a picnic" and not "lost in the woods." Perhaps most important, however, is that we encourage and embrace student individuality. We reject the fear associated with being unique or being "out there" . We recognize that it takes courage to openly advocate for a "crazy" idea. Sometimes, crazy ideas lead to world-changing innovations. I plainly state that students are being assessed, tested, prodded, surveyed, and scored to an insane degree in our schools. We attempt to find ways to categorize students to see how they "stack up" against their peers. That is all a way of asking the student "How intelligent are you?" To the contrary, I pronounce that THIS class is about asking a very different question with the exact same words:

How are *YOU* intelligent?

The rephrasing does much to dramatize the difference and emphasize the importance of what makes us unique. There is no way that we cannot be unique to each other. None of us were raised the exact same way with the exact same formative (and non-formative) experiences. As unique patchwork quilts of life experiences, we have aspects of ourselves and competencies we excel at that become part of our unique fingerprint of qualities which make us a viable contributor to the world and a player on the world stage. It may be a bit part. It may be a lead role. But you can and should contribute to the performance happening daily once you've found your voice.

> O me! O life! . . . of the questions of these recurring; of the endless trains of the faithless . . . of cities filled with the foolish; what good amid these, O me, O life? Answer: that you are here; that life exists, and identity; that the powerful play goes on and you may contribute a verse; that the powerful play goes on and you may contribute a verse. What will your verse be?
>
> Walt Whitman[6]

Returning to my undergraduate experience with classmates full of vim and vigor, I have a shocking admission: despite the fact that we thought we knew everything, we really did not. Hard to believe. We were greenhorn trainees on a ship together navigating our collective paths and collaborating on collective artworks together for four tough years. Despite our vast differences and aesthetic sensibilities, we gradually learned that combining forces had the biggest impact on ourselves and each other. But we quickly learned that we had little experience in collaborating, little understanding of what our collective voices should say together, and little knowledge of how to say it.

When I was mentoring student designers, I had a faculty professional director explain the often-frustrating situation in which he found herself with student designers: a design meeting takes place, the piece is discussed, and all the wonderful "what if's" are shared. Conversations center around what the play says to a modern-day audience and the reasons for including the piece in the overall season. Perhaps design elements are broadly and generally discussed like ingredients in a recipe related to shadows or colors or shapes or all of the above. Hopes are high for what we can all together accomplish!

Given guidance, designers disperse again to their respective studio kitchen tables and assimilate thoughts from the discussion. The notes spread before you, the same fear that accompanied the clawing and scratching phase may return and perhaps morph into a sense of dread or a mild case of imposter syndrome. What did we talk about exactly? How do I combine thoughts from that meeting and my research and perhaps some preliminary sketches into . . . something? At least I've got this list of ingredients . . .

Inevitably, the designers would come back with amalgamations that represented what he said he thought he wanted, but when combined, just did not work well. A preliminary design was introduced that is essentially the combination of the ingredients mentioned at the first meeting aesthetically cooked into a design stew. The student designer believed that their job was to simply take the elements mentioned in the first conversation and, regardless of taste, mix them together and present them as a design. "You said you liked bright colors and stick shapes while referencing multiple levels so here's a jungle-gym of yellow pipes with platforms . . ." None of the *designer* is in that stew! Just the ingredients mixed together.

The first meeting was interpreted as a recipe session and not an opportunity to generate new ideas from that conversation. Here was your chance to defer on your own humility and add you—and your own talents—to the whole of the experience. To draw on the chemistry lab analogy again, you did add chemicals together as instructed, but your own intuition was left out of the process. To add that requires self-confidence often lacking in a young designer, but that is the secret sauce of the entire recipe! To not add that is to negate your contribution to the design process and minimize what is an essential component to collaboration. Six different artists in a room conceiving of a production together will inherently craft a different production than six different artists in another room—or perhaps five of the *same* artists with a new one added into the mix. In each case, the process and the product are different. One of the beautiful aspects of the collaborative artform we call theatre is that each time a script is picked up by a different company dedicating themselves to that work, a new and vibrant magic unique to *that* production with *that* team is created unlike any production of the same script that came before it or that will follow. Think about the alchemy of that moment and the type of magic that collaboration with new voices can create! The same exact words on a page are crafted into a unique experience every time a new team of artists sit down to make a production out of those words. That a single tree can imbue thousands of different and unique branches from the same trunk is, at its essence, what is a uniquely human experience tied to our unique ability to see that which does not yet exist but can with our combined ingenuity and creativity.

> We had taken up aeronautics merely as a sport.
> We reluctantly entered upon the scientific side of it.
>
> Orville Wright[7]

Q-Theory and the Creative Team

In 2005, Brian Uzzi, Professor of Management and Organizations at the Kellogg School of Management at Northwestern University published a study after becoming obsessed over one question: what's the makeup of the teams that produce the most successful Broadway shows?[8] In conjunction with Jarrett Spiro of Stanford University, the two studied the creative teams of 2,258 Broadway musicals produced from 1877 to 1990. The study set out to prove a theory that teams of collaborative artists who had worked together multiple times on multiple Broadway productions were more likely to produce a successful show than a team working together—and with each other—for the first time. Each of the more than 2,000 shows over that period of time were assigned a Q score (Q = Cluster Coefficient over Average Path Length).[9] Productions comprised of teams with a high Q score meant that the cast and production teams knew each other well and had collaborated with each other on some earlier production or productions. The study did determine that the lower the Q score, the less likely it was that the show would be successful (at the box office), but another revealing truth came to light which contradicted the hypothesis going into the study: productions with Q scores in the middle range were actually most likely to be successful.[10] Productions with the highest Q score were NOT the most—successful productions were comprised of creative teams which had one or two creative team members who were new to the team. Uzzi surmised that the influx of new ideas from a new team member breathes life into a creative team (and therefore the production) which energizes and pushes the envelope on the collective idea-making avoiding what social scientists call "groupthink."[11]

Not unlike successful and dynastic teams in the world of sports, successful collaborative teams inevitably involve a mixture of established Broadway "legend" talent and new rookie voices that add vitality and new ideas to the collaborative enterprise.

The Q-theory study is a lesson in maintaining a vibrant dynamic in creative teams. Recognizing the value of new team members and the perspective and diversity of ideas they bring to the table is an important lesson in collaboration of any kind inside or outside the theatre business.

Consider the team or teams you have assembled on projects or ones for which you yourself have been a member. Did the team reach a stasis of groupthink only to be revitalized by a new perspective and a valuable questioning of assumptions?

In the context of this chapter, the lesson here is: speak up! It takes courage, arguably more so when the creative team is comprised of successful artists who have worked together before with you as the exception. Remind yourself that you are there for a reason: to add a new voice that speaks for a perhaps previously unspoken or ignored segment of the population or a desperately needed new voice with a cultural and racial perspective not included in the other team members. Who knows? Your unique voice and artistic lens may prompt a reframe of the entire production.

The only way to be certain that won't happen is to say nothing and contribute little beyond a combination of ingredients to the theatrical recipe. So, don't! Speak up! You are part of the alchemy that makes that production unique.

Design as Collaborative Craft

We designers are products of our mentors and they a product of theirs. Stage designing is a craft that is as much making-and-doing as it is the result of study of the work of our predecessors. We stand on the shoulders of designers that came before us, but with a reverence for them and the trailblazing in the art form that they created. In fact, I remembered the Zeffirelli "air vibration" story when I had a bit of an "Ah-ha" moment designing a low-budget production of Chekhov's *Seagull* at the Marin Theatre Company a number of years ago and did my best to channel the great man. The set transformed as the play went on to have birch trees that intersected and framed the space in a way that felt more and more like a cage than a vista of birch trees in a bleak Russian landscape (see plate 15).

What's more, Zeffirelli may have appreciated the simplest of methods by which the birch tree tubes were moved along stretched lines—eight rods and reels with stretched fishing lines across the stage. Never caught a fish the entire run, but we were able to create some marvelous stage pictures and gestures (see plate 17).

This ability to see things that are not there and dream up ideas that do not exist yet is a power—a real POWER pure and simple. Combining those dreams with others is like jet fuel for the creative process. Nothing at all in the theatre happens in a vacuum. Without the artists and technicians up and down the line of the production team, *none* of what you design will ever come to light. To dream up a world and have a team of people help you and the director bring that world to life is a privilege plain and simple. Never forget that.

7

The Tech and Preview Process—the Ultimate Proof-of-Concept

Chapter Outline

Recognize Your Role

On some occasions during my undergraduate experience, the magic of the upstairs theatre and the arduous theatrical training in the downstairs basement classroom met in what would become some of the most memorable lectures of my college career. Talented designers would spend an hour talking about the production happening upstairs on the stage. For me, one thing made these talks memorable looking past the obvious fact that these were real living-breathing professional designers taking a break from practicing the craft we students were passionately interested in learning: their honesty. Their honesty. Simple as that. Just honesty. As they had no particular ties to the university and no real obligation to sugarcoat the message, each designer could just say the few words or sentences that they wish they themselves had heard as undergraduate college students.

For example, there was Scenic Designer Michael Ganio (now at Dartmouth University) who imparted his wisdom softly as if spoken by a therapist in a quiet office with nothing but a clock ticking. He calmly stated: "I am *amazed* at how far you can get in this business just by being on time and competent."[1] It is the little things, the subtle details, the "if you're not early, you're late" idea that landed with that one bit of theatrical truth. People have been gracious enough to believe in you and your contribution to the work. Who are we to disrespect our fellow creative team members by not showing up on time and not having something to contribute to the conversation? Could be a bit of provocative research or a quote that is a catalyst for a design conversation. Just being "on time and competent" goes a very long way.

In another visit, Costume Designer Marie Ann Chiment (now at Temple University) bluntly told the assembled class: "If you don't like working with people, do something else."[2] She went on to explain that "in this business, the designer is always the buffer between a director who wants more and a shop that has had enough."[3] Theatre is a team art form, but a designer must recognize their role on that team. At times, we are thrust into the role of mediator between two parties: the director and the shops we essentially represent. The result is a delicate and difficult balancing act that must factor in the time, budget, and human resources needed to complete or perhaps redo/redesign an element of the show.

If it's a redesign and it is because you overlooked something on the drawings, you can be sure that you will be the one the shop is grumbling about when they are fixing your mistake with a crowbar when it should have been an eraser. And that happens to ALL of us no matter our skill level. I have been known to overlook important lines on drawings that indicate a height restriction offstage only to find ourselves chopping some scenery down with a saw and a lot of complaining once the set is full-scale and changes are costly and embarrassing. On lots of days and at lots of times, the job is not a fun one and is certainly not glamourous. Particularly during the technical rehearsal process, nerves are frayed, and everyone is pushed to their limit. In those moments, trying to negotiate between the two sides almost always means you are in the middle by default. Be aware that comes with the job and you must resort to humility and kindness when it does.

With certainty, every production pendulum swings back to collaboration with others and negotiation on multiple levels with multiple viewpoints from budget to feasibility to accessibility. There are the inevitable ruffled feathers and hurt feelings. And it is here when Marie Ann Chiment's simple and profoundly truthful advice (while she herself was in tech rehearsals) rings true:

> Not only is collaboration "key," it is the rest of the door, the rooms, the neighbor's house . . . everything!
>
> You. Must. Collaborate.

With dignity, humility, and with an eye towards the bigger picture of which you are only a piece: that's the deal. That's the contract. It's not either/or. Succeed and you'll have a front row seat for:

1. The thrill of creating a production with other artists who make *your* work better.
2. Sharing in the joy that comes from combining talents in a way that makes the collective work exponentially more visceral and profound to an audience because it represents a *combination* of ideas built on top of other ideas,
3. The payoff of having an audience appreciate the way a story came to life and . . .
4. The built-in support system that is there when an audience does not.

A Musical Factory with Lessons to Spare

For four straight summers, I had the opportunity to design ten shows at the Muny in St Louis. Short for "municipal," the Muny is a unique representation of theatre for the people by the people and it operates on a vast scale both in terms of staff and space. The theatre has a stage width of about ninety feet and a stage depth of fifty-plus feet. Sitting in the middle is a forty-seven-foot diameter revolving stage bisected by two gigantic "boom" walls that cross the stage at roughly eighty and seventy feet in width each that are a massive twenty-three feet high. Despite the vast stage and the massive scale of the scenery, the entirety of the stage looks like a toy from the back of an 11,000-seat house where 1,500 seats are free to the public. On any given night during the summer, crowds will assemble at the top of the hill at the back of the theatre, have a picnic, share some music, and line up for a free seat. For some, it's the first time they have seen a musical in their lives. At the bottom of the hill is an historic and awe-inspiring stage where the likes of Robert Goulet, Ann Margaret, and Rob McClure have all toe-tapped and sung to the delight of thousands in a single night. Shows began on that spot in 1917 with a production of *As You Like It* in the middle of a grove of trees at the base of a hill—a twentieth-century equivalent of the Theatre of Dionysus with seating built into the natural hillside.

For over 100 years and counting, the Muny has been a factory for musicals in the summer. Seven musicals are mounted and performed over a period of about eight weeks from mid-June to mid-August. Shows only run about a week to ten days given the fact that it does not take long to burn through a subscription base when you have 11,000 seats in the auduence. Like Packers tickets, seats are handed down generation-to-generation and included as gifts in wills from one family member to another. At any given time, a show will be in performance onstage and two to three more that follow in the season are in-process on the backlot behind the stage with music, choreography, and staging rehearsals happening in adjoining buildings and outdoor platforms nearby. These musical "factory workers" have an entirely shared experience all-summer with Broadway actors in tank tops and tights dining at outdoor benches side-by-side with local St. Louis scenic artists wearing cut-off overalls emblematic of a patchwork quilt of multiple seasons of shows from all around the city. Ask about a splotch and you'll hear something along the lines of "This one here is from *Man of La Mancha* four seasons ago and this one was from that disastrous *Peter Pan* we did in '98" … remember? …" Watching these artists at work standing with brushes, chalk, and markers connected to a simple bamboo stick with a rubber band can be a sight to behold. They represent generations of scenic artists who regularly come back to the Muny to spend a summer painting with about sixteen of their fellow artist brothers and sisters along with a couple of apprentices who spend a lot of time washing buckets and mixing colors. A massive eighty feet wide by twenty-three feet tall "boom" drop can have as many as a dozen scenic artists crafting a stunning image in a matter of days. That giant piece of scenery represents only a small piece of the theatrical puzzle put together on the stage about 100 feet away (see plate 16).

Similar mastery is displayed in every area of this backstage factory in all facets from lighting to carpentry to props and with lightning speed. The average build time is only about seven to ten days from start-to-finish.

As a designer, the day begins precisely at 7am and goes until about 7pm with a production meeting at the end of each day. Take *Seussical* as an example where comments like the following are not all that uncommon:

> The actor playing Horton-the-Elephant has bad knees and the "nest" (crafted from a papasan chair frame found for free on Craigslist) needs an additional

> six inches of height and some kind of braking device because it's getting kind of squirrely on him when he sits on it ... and where does the tiny piano come from that Cat-in-the-Hat plays? Is that on wheels? And does that come out of the in-1 entrance or in-2 because in-3 is too far upstage? ...
>
> Oh and we need the blunderbuss guns in rehearsal ASAP if those are still in the show ... (See plate 18.)

The entire summer feels like a race that you never quite finish. A designer may come in at 7am thinking that they have all day to get that one drawing done, but at 7:01am chaos may erupt. The phone rings and it's the Props Director looking over the notes compiled from the previous night's production meeting:

> What the F is this about a blunderbuss gun? What the hell does that look like? If they want it now, you're going to have to come down here and cobble something together for us to replicate ...

An entire visual history of the Muny spanning decades exists in the basement catacombs of the prop warehouse from barrels of halberds to piles of baskets to about seven different varieties of ceremonial thrones. Objects in this environment are not and never were precious to anyone. In general, they are grotesquely exaggerated, scaled-up representations of objects given that the closest audience member is about thirty feet away and the farthest is much farther. The necessity of making a blunderbuss gun out of found objects means having the mind of a child, to an extent. What can we cobble together that looks like something Seussian from thirty feet or more away? Legendary designer Desmond Heeley was famously asked in a shop once about the need for "flowers" to adorn the canopy bed for a production of *Beauty and the Beast*. Having just taken a break, the carpenters had arranged a table for coffee with all the usual plasticware and condiments needed for making a good cup of coffee. Desmond grabbed three spoons out of a paper cup sitting on the table, fanned them out between his thumb and forefinger and replied, "make me 200 of these and spray paint them gold."

It was with this eye-of-a-child and a channeling of everyone's inner Dr Seuss and Desmond Heeley that we hastily assembled a blunderbuss gun using an existing plywood cutout of a rifle with a funnel attached to the end and some curly bits taped to it found in a drawer marked "lamp parts" capped off with a plastic horn off a child's bicycle. "Done! ... now make ten more."

There is a shoot-from-the-hip style of decision-making and craft that exists by necessity and permeates almost all aspects of the Muny operation. Creativity is perhaps less of a choice and more of a means of survival each day. Time is in short supply and virtually all decisions are made based in some sense on what can be reasonably achieved in the shortest amount of time. Speed is the heartbeat of the organization during the summer as mounting seven full musicals in eight weeks is a somewhat insane undertaking. On any given day, a piece of scenery might be cut or even in the three hours between the final onstage rehearsal (affectionately called a "sweat tech" because it takes place from noon to 5pm on a muggy St. Louis summer day) and opening night beginning at 8pm that evening. If something just "isn't working" and the best way to eliminate error means eliminating the piece that took time to design/build/paint, then eliminate it they will.

At age sixteen, I had a job as a busboy at a Bennigan's restaurant for about twenty minutes. After a few weeks of filing people's drinks and breaking more than my fair share of dishes, I resolved myself to the notion that a job I sought in life would have to be unique—a job where "every day was different." The widget-making life was not for me. The Muny is certainly that! The experience is fun, but a grind as well. Time, or the lack thereof, creates an anxious combination of nervousness and thrill-seeking craft-making. Many ideas are not even tested until 11,000 people see it with you on an opening night.

The Marie Ann Chiment rule applies here as well only with less time available: directors will want more, and the crew will be at maximum exhaustion. If you draw the short straw as a designer, you might be assigned to the seventh show of a seven-show season when nerves are frayed and a summer of construction in the sweltering heat has taken its toll. And I am, by no means, an authority on keeping my cool in the heat of those (heated) discussions. I speak with experience from both sides of the argument. Theatre is a pressure cooker already. Theatre on a reduced timeframe with an exhausted group of collaborators crafting multiple shows at once is a pressure cooker that inevitably boils over at times.

The job of the designer for those twelve hours each day is to try and answer a whirlwind of questions (often with visuals that may or may not exist at the time the question is being asked) all day for a large chunk of the day in service to multiple departments. Thousands of pages of tracking sheets are printed representing plan views of the movements of multiple pieces of scenery. These sheets are our best way to track scenery movements and identify problems on paper before they are problems with people (translation: crew waiting for you to tell them where to move something and when).

There is a bit of a "flying the plane as you build it" energy to it all. The intent is that, when the magical technical rehearsal time comes, all the pieces will come together beautifully, the plane will fly, and we send the show on its way. As my Muny colleagues would likely agree, that has likely *never* happened in the 100+ years of the theatre's existence. There are always setbacks and surprises that complicate the effort (and these all actually happened):

1. The actor playing the Beast in *Beauty and the Beast* is already tall at about 6'-6". He is costumed in a top hat that makes him even taller. By itself, that's not an issue, but how tall is the door he enters at the top of Act One, Scene 4?
2. Metal grating on a fire escape for *West Side Story* seems the perfect material for both the look and the ability to light through the surface both above and below, but what if Maria is in high heels?
3. The Wicked Witch in *The Wizard of Oz* had a giant book of spells (an old phone book) on a table in her witch's chambers ... until a pyrotechnics cue sends a glowing ember into it and sets it on fire.

Around a card table with everyone all-in on a bet is a bad time to begin evaluating your chances. The process of installing a production into a theatre is a bet based on hours and hours of careful planning and preparation in multiple areas from acting rehearsals to tests of automation to experiments with sound and lighting. Sometimes we win, sometimes we lose. And getting the plane off the ground will require some lift from multiple sources regardless of any built-in aerodynamics.

The Leap of Faith

The technical rehearsal is a leap of faith on the wings of an idea that multiple people have invested in all at once. Like any business, a production is a project with a limited amount of time and money. Our "deadline" is opening night and our "deliverables" include a combination of both human talent in the form of actors "selling our product" (the show) in the context of a surrounding "building" (the set) meant to make you believe that an entirely new and perhaps fantastical world has unfolded in front of you hatched out of a hand-crafted machine that is part time-capsule and part portal to another universe.

The creative process in the theatrical realm is a study in contrasts:

On the one hand, you have unique and talented individuals who have a goal to create art, make a name for themselves in that space, and become—as individual artists—sought after for their talents in their specific area of expertise on a creative team. Put the right team together and you are likely to have a successful production. The desire to excel and be recognized for artistic contributions is, of course, in every artist's DNA. It moves us to work harder, do more research, visualize our ideas more fully, and develop our artistic voice. If we were athletes, we would have our personal heroes and want to play like they do. It is no different for the theatre artist to dream of becoming the next Broadway designer with the recognition that comes with that role and that position.

On the other hand, collaboration is key! No collaborative artist can expect to simultaneously produce, write, direct, design, act, and market the show no matter how many times we have felt that way or played those individual roles in our lifetime. Do not act like that's the case. In these moments a designer must be selfless enough to let go of a sacred-cow idea that has perhaps been with them from the beginning. In a sense, it is in this phase that you must simultaneously stand both inside and outside of yourself as if you are a spirit floating above the situation and able to see clearly the good ideas from the ones that don't belong.

Know your role when it comes to these two expectations. Know when to flip between the two. At times, it will be multiple times in the same two-hour meeting. That is not an exaggeration. I have often wished it were. To genuinely collaborate means, as the saying goes, "a high tide rises all boats." The work is blatantly and unapologetically both self*ish* and self*less* at the same time. As a member of a creative team, you must be the cheerleader for good ideas no matter who came up with them and be willing to accept criticism of your own work when it does not suit the mission or vision of the production being created. Know a good idea when you hear one and be humble enough to recognize it and adopt it as a touchstone in the design process moving forward when circumstances warrant that. The production puzzle is a complicated one. Be careful not to complicate it further with hubris or a false sense of a recognition you believe you deserve.

To over-simplify, let's say that you and your collaborators are collectively painting a portrait. Since the first reading of the words used to describe the subject of the portrait, you have been convinced that red must be a component of that portrait. Other colors are held by other creative team members, and they are crafting a portrait that they all believe in and recognize as emblematic of the description. And red just does not fit. They know it and, if you could float above the mêlée and see it for yourself with a clarity of vision, you would know it as well. But, more often than not, you are not floating above (unless you have powers of which I am unaware) and clarity is muddied by the history of this choice—that red just *had* to be in this painting. The good of the whole and the integrity of the painting you are collaboratively making must always take priority. You may be nodding your head now and saying "of course" under your breath, but you and I both know that putting this advice into practice is a bumpy ride and never easy.

When it all works, when it all comes together, when collaborative artists both cede territory to other collaborators and add their piece of the aircraft to the mix, the result can be a thrilling ride unique to this artform we call theatre.

The Playwright as Prophet

Some years ago, I was hired to complete an amazing creative team for a 2004 production of *Major Barbara* at the San Jose Repertory Theatre. The play itself is as prophetic as they come, written by a playwright who not only tapped into what it means to be moral and the variability of morality but foresaw what President Dwight D. Eisenhower would call the "military industrial complex" about fifty years before those words were first uttered. Written 100 years before our production in 1905, the play centers around a matronly Salvation Army director named Barbara and her father, Andrew Undershaft, a weapons manufacturer who delights in selling weapons and making money. While Barbara clings to her devout Christian faith to guide her in her efforts to help those in need who pass through her doors at the Salvation Army, she finds herself in an achingly familiar moral dilemma for anyone who has ever questioned the source of funds that not only keep their organization alive, but also poke at the fabric of the principles upon which that organization was founded. In Barbara's case, her father wants to give her money to save her beloved shelter. Barbara's faith and the belief that it is her duty to *save* lives flies in the face of her own father's faith which he proudly proclaims is:

> To give arms to all men who offer an honest price for them, without respect of persons or principles: to aristocrat and republican, to Nihilist and Tsar, to

Capitalist and Socialist, to Protestant and Catholic, to burglar and policeman, to black man, white man and yellow man, to all sorts and conditions, all nationalities, all faiths, all follies, all causes and all crimes. [4]

In an exchange with his own son, Undershaft admits what could be considered sacrilege to a member of the Salvation Army: that there is no one true morality:

STEPHEN [coldly—almost sullenly] You speak as if there were half a dozen moralities and religions to choose from, instead of one true morality and one true religion.

UNDERSHAFT. For me there is only one true morality; but it might not fit you, as you do not manufacture aerial battleships. There is only one true morality for every man; but every man has not the same true morality.[5]

At the time that we did the play, our country was mired in what many believed to be a war of choice in Iraq and an abuse of power by those in charge of instigating it. Motives were being questioned as to the why's underlying the reasons for engaging in it. The Vice President himself maintained ties to the twenty-first century equivalent of Andrew Undershaft's own company in Halliburton—a weapons manufacturer and distributor. A war of choice with American blood on the battlefield made all of us question our motives for starting the war in the first place and reviving George Bernard Shaw's play seemed the best way to share a 100-year-old story with an audience with a lens sharply focused on our current role as a country in the Middle East. Why were we there and was it solely to blow things up and sell more weapons?

Shaw's stage directions for settings are famously detailed, seemingly down to the brand of the cigarette nub tossed into the detritus downstage left. As is often the case, many designers (myself included) tend to ignore those directions in an effort to not be influenced by any prescribed method of designing the piece for a new audience in a new era. At stake is not only the integrity of the production, but also the originality of the work.

So, we proceed with the process of creating three giant settings across three big acts in the play: Lady Britomart's library, a Salvation Army yard, and finally, in Act III, Scene 2, a Undershaft munitions works in Perivale St. Andrews described in agonizing detail by Shaw as:

Perivale St Andrews lies between two Middlesex hills, half climbing the northern one. It is an almost smokeless town of white walls, roofs of narrow green slates or red tiles, tall trees, domes, campaniles, and slender chimney

> shafts, beautifully situated and beautiful in itself. The best view of it is obtained from the crest of a slope about half a mile to the east, where the high explosives are dealt with. The foundry lies hidden in the depths between, the tops of its chimneys sprouting like huge skittles into the middle distance. Across the crest runs a platform of concrete, with a parapet which suggests a fortification, because there is a huge cannon of the obsolete Woolwich Infant pattern peering across it at the town. The cannon is mounted on an experimental gun carriage: possibly the original model of the Undershaft disappearing rampart gun alluded to by Stephen. The parapet has a high step inside which serves as a seat.[6]

(There is more, but I'll spare you the rest.)

Despite the care with which Shaw describes what he *prescribes* you design for Act III, Scene 2, we were moved by those two words "aerial battleship" and their juxtaposition to a pair of important and relevant dates:

1 Shaw premiered the play in 1905 and published it in 1907.
2 In 1903, just two years before, two bicycle mechanics known as the Wright Brothers had taken their first flight in an aircraft on the North Carolina coast.

With air travel in its infancy, Shaw had already extrapolated that man's baby step towards domination of the skies above cities would, combined with our unfortunate tendency to want to dominate other countries on the ground, meant that we would find a way to adapt flight as a tool of war and create a battlefield in the sky. Shaw's pen was prophetic. The phrase "aerial battleship" appears in the play five times as he describes the success of the plane itself as an instrument of death regardless of who is involved in the conflict. He answers a question about who won a battle with the following:

> UNDERSHAFT. Oh, I don't know. Which side wins does not concern us here. No: the good news is that the aerial battleship is a tremendous success. At the first trial it has wiped out a fort with three hundred soldiers in it.[7]

The creative team returns again to the "What if . . ." and we reframe Act III, Scene 2 at Perivale St. Andrews as the parking spot for a massive aerial battleship designed with a nod not to how bomber aircraft will look, but how they might look to Andrew Undershaft and his designers in 1905. It looked like the lovechild of H.G. Wells *War of the Worlds* and DaVinci's flying machines:

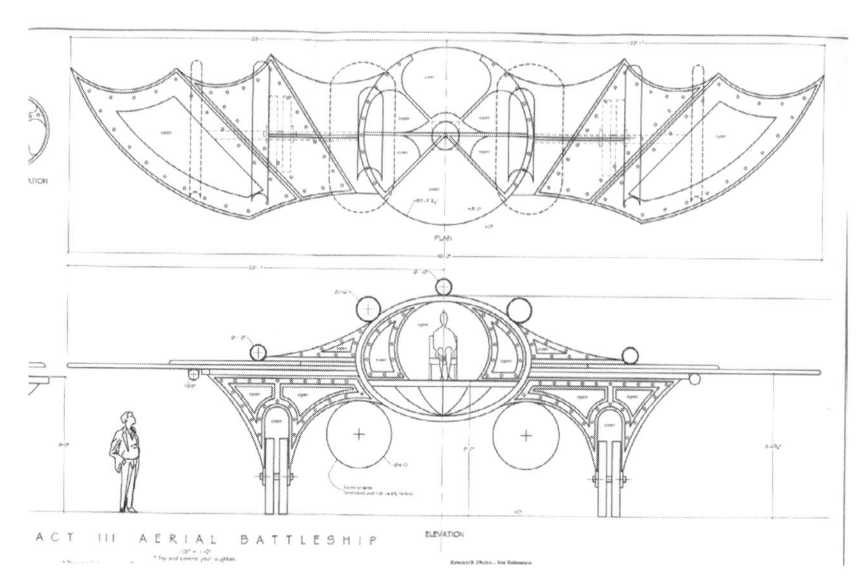

Figure 7.1 Design/Drawings of early Nineteenth-century "Aerial Battleship" for *Major Barbara*. *Source: design/drawings by author.*

(See plate 19).

At just over forty-six feet in width from wingtip to wingtip, the plane was massive and designed to be a shiny black with gold rivets. While it is one thing hatch an idea that leads to a design of this kind, it is quite another to coordinate the technical elements to pull off an idea of this scale from construction to installation. The result was a technically choreographed epic scene change from Lady Britomart's library to a reveal of the aircraft sitting just behind a large drop with aircraft landing lights mounted under the wings. Every second of that shift had to be coordinated with other departments—lighting, costumes, sound, shifting scenery, etc. Dialogue between departments had to happen months in advance to be sure our collective foray into the spectacle of the aerial battleship would not only provoke awe in the audiences that witnessed it, but also perform what the director wanted of it once the reveal of our menacing weapon of war had concluded; among them, she wanted actors to walk on it. Every good design must serve a utilitarian and a visual purpose. One without the other is "one hand clapping."

But lo the marvelous feeling when it *all comes together*!

The Promise of the Payoff

When a team of artists start with two words: "aerial battleship" and a vison, anything is possible! From first meeting to testing out the invention in the glorious laboratory of ideas called the technical rehearsal, we witnessed our collective efforts with the anticipation of a baby being born. Will it look and feel and resound inside of our souls the way we hoped it would seated around a table nine months earlier with an idea and a dream? Would an investment of time, manpower, and money from up to 100 or so individuals up and down the line of creation culminate into one startling and raw visual statement to an audience of our fellow human beings: that in order for weapons to be useful and lucrative they have to be used. We must not overlook that the manufacturers of such instruments of death have "one true morality" to wealth and that they count success in lifeless bodies and monetary gains. Every production worth doing has a poignant statement at its core built on a story that transcends the time in which it was written.

It is at THIS moment that we theatre dreamers realize our true calling! We realize that we are mystics who craft magic together as a means of holding up a mirror to society and asking, "Is this who we are?" followed closely on the heels of that question with "Is this who we want to be?"

Months of meetings and emails and visuals and phone calls about this single moment onstage all seem worth it when an actor enters the library in costume and begins to orchestrate the transition under a growing drumbeat that slowly builds, followed by smoke and a mighty shifting of light. A wall of books rises to the heavens, props are shifted off, smoke clears, and a large upstage drop goes up to reveal—with a cymbal crash—a massive aerial battleship with lights pointed directly at the audience. For a blinding moment, you think the aircraft is rolling downstage towards you! A tingling on the back of your neck tells you that it is indeed what you all envisioned together—perhaps *better*.

THAT is the payoff fellow troubadours of the stage!

THAT is why we do it.

THAT is the theatre gods and the spirits of the theatre masters who came before us noting the occasion and whispering: "well done—look at what you did *together*."

And it is precisely that moment that the clock begins again: new productions come along, new creative teams are formed, and the desire begins again to find another group of restless souls who want to boldly tell a story worth telling an audience willing to experience it.

8

The Inevitability of Failure and the Sea of Criticism

Chapter Outline

Courage: The Man (or Woman or Person) in the Arena

> The business of theatre demands you have a completely fortified heart to withstand all the rejection, but the craft of theatre demands your heart be wide open so to create vulnerability and truth. And the effort of sustaining both states is. . .a lot
>
> Paco Tolson[1]

Being a theatrical artist asks a lot of an individual: referencing the duality I mentioned earlier, you must be both a sorcerer AND an apprentice. I have had the privilege of being both in my theatre career. As with any creative process, I am constantly learning and constantly plying/trying/experimenting and often failing in almost every endeavor.

To ask parents or relatives what they think of a young designer's choice to "become an artist" or "become a designer" and the response is often some variation of "Oh ... that's nice" and typically followed up with some variation of "So what are you going to DO with that degree/skill/etc?" The truth is that it takes a great deal of personal courage to "make a go" of life as a young theatre designer or a young fine artist. It takes IMMENSE courage to dare greatly.

> It is not the critic who counts; not the man who points out how the strong man stumbles, or where the doer of deeds could have done them better. The credit belongs to the man who is actually in the arena, whose face is marred by dust and sweat and blood; who strives valiantly; who errs, who comes short again and again, because there is no effort without error and shortcoming; but who does actually strive to do the deeds; who knows great enthusiasms, the great devotions; who spends himself in a worthy cause; who at the best knows in the end the triumph of high achievement, and who at the worst, if he fails, at least fails while daring greatly, so that his place shall never be with those cold and timid souls who neither know victory nor defeat.
>
> Theodore Roosevelt[2]

What inevitably follows for a young designer is a period of time that can—and often does—strike at the crux of an individual's will fed by thoughts of self-doubt, uncertainty, and perhaps even shame, for having the audacity to pursue a life that, to others, seems a journey of folly and an adventure with completely unknown consequences. Others see you as jumping without the security of a net beneath you.

People forget that adventures don't always end well. In 1921, British explorer Ernest Shackleton led a team on an expedition to the Antarctic only to die in the process. The point is that adventures (of all kinds) are fraught with uncertainties and clouded in doubt. It is the intrepid artistic explorer who chooses to board that ship knowing that it may perhaps take them to where they want to go but not without some tossing and rocking along the way.

To pile on, there is often a sense that the artist is not fulfilling his or her true potential or that the entire IDEA is merely a cry for help or a selfish display of blind bravado that, to others, looks like a "phase" that will pass before the aforementioned artist is forced to seek out and take a "real job" when it comes along. It is important to recognize, for those that have tried it and those who watch from the sidelines, that daring to be an artist can be the most selfless and most courageous act. It was not that long ago that the word "creativity" was a mildly condescending term. Some speak to an aspiring artist as if they were a person from a foreign land: "How nice that you can express your creativity in that way." The truth is that now "creativity" has become a buzzword in the lexicon of arts leaders and business leaders alike.

Perhaps, after all these years and like a banished king returning to their homeland to sit in the place of power once again, the word "creativity" has become a respected term that conveys so many different meanings to so many different people. The good news is that, in some circles, it may be replacing the condescension that once existed in the non-artistic community for the term and recognizing the magic powers it possesses. Artists now seem to have some kind of "it factor" in their creativity that is useful to others.

In an article for the New York Times, Janet Rae-Dupree quotes Daniel Pink's phrase "The MFA [master of fine arts] is the new MBA". This has taken hold in many circles from Harvard Business to Fast Company and Forbes. As with anything, there is a danger of creativity being considered a catch-all remedy for what may ail your company. A simple online search yields references for the word that, in any other time period, could be replaced with something along the lines of "magical elixir." The internet is the medicine man for this new drug.

Do no Harm, Take no Shit

In *The Sketches of Frank Gehry*, Pollack asks Gehry a simple question: "Is starting hard?"[4] Gehry's response is classic artistic avoidance that should comfort—and not scare—every young designer:

> You know it is. I don't know what you do when you start, but I clean my desk, I make a lot of stupid appointments that I make sound important. Avoidance, delay, denial. I'm always scared that I'm not going to know what to do. It's a terrifying moment. And then when I start, I'm always amazed: "Oh, that wasn't so bad."[5]

Like all of us, Frank Gehry fears the beginning of a new project and the uncertainty that surrounds that menacing blank page before him. As I tell my own students and, more importantly, myself on multiple occasions, "If Frank *Freaking* Gehry fears the blank page, then it is completely fine for all artists to feel that way as well." It is entirely, understandably, and completely *normal*. Fear is inevitable. The sooner you get past the fear and come to peace with the notion that you may (let's face it) fail at whatever you're trying to do, the sooner you'll reach a place where failure is OK always. In military circles, perhaps you'd call it "an acceptable risk." The fact is that even Frank Gehry feels this way should mean something to the young designer worried about the line of judges awaiting the artistic work of ANY flavor to be displayed, judged, and (perhaps) flop. Because that's life. That IS and always SHOULD BE an acceptable risk. If not, an artist cannot call themselves an artist.

A journalist at a press conference once asked Gehry himself if his own "emblematic buildings" were just about spectacle. Gehry's response was simple. He calmly held up his middle finger.

> A long silence followed before a different reporter asked whether "emblematic buildings" such as his would continue to be a feature of modern cities.
>
> "Let me tell you one thing," he replied. "In this world we are living in, 98% of everything that is built and designed today is pure shit. There's *no* sense of design, no respect for humanity or for anything else. They are damn buildings and that's it.
>
> "Once in a while, however, a group of people do something special. Very few, but God, leave us alone. We are dedicated to our work. I don't ask for work . . . I work with clients who respect the art of architecture. Therefore, please don't ask questions as stupid as that one."[6]

While perhaps thought to be disrespectful on the surface, Gehry's response to the question has so many levels to explore:

Listen to your Own Muse . . . and Follow it Despite Criticism

Like his work or not, Gehry does not care. He cares about doing his work, for his clients (who do like his work) and on his terms. He has spent years being ridiculed for work that is often called "ugly" or "emblematic". His response is always that his buildings mean something to him and his clients. His buildings, for him, are an emotional response to space and a crafting of volume that is unlike any other architecture seen before or since. His response is, interestingly enough, emblematic of his devotion to his craft and his aesthetic.

Spectacle Redefined

For Gehry, the term "spectacle" means there is no there there. No soul to the work and no effort to craft truly unique and inspiring works of art that, in this case, sit in a category called architecture—a category that often prioritizes utility over all else. His contention is that spectacle is (and literally was in this case) an accusation that his work lacked a central aesthetic soul. That accusation is an insult to Gehry and prompted a response commensurate with that accusation—the middle finger.

Accept the Unaccepted

Van Gogh's work was criticized throughout his entire artistic life. Consider this: he sold a SINGLE painting in his lifetime equal to just $1,000 today. His work weathered storms of insults as vibrant and violent as his own paintings: it was called "amateur" as well as "strange, intense, and feverish." Today his paintings can fetch over $60 million. So, what's to be learned here? Van Gogh accepted (but not without angst and woe) the fact that his work would not be recognized as great during his lifetime. He persevered knowing that what he was creating was, by all accounts now in hindsight, truly "ahead of its time." A modern artist has every right to dispute that. After all, one cannot pay the rent by producing works that never sell and that is a very valid point. Gehry's point, while dismissive, also highlights the fact that he does his work for himself. His own home was a radical—and highly criticized at the time—departure from the norms of what an architect is *supposed* to do. But, like Van Gogh, he did it anyway. He was thinking with his hands and crafting an aesthetic and a muse to which he has remained true throughout his career.

> "All great works of art are trophies of victorious struggle."
>
> Julius Meier-Graefe[7]

A Moon for the Misbegotten and the Very Public Failure

In 2005, I had just designed my second show at the prestigious American Conservatory Theatre (ACT) in San Francisco, California. Designing in the historic Geary Theatre in downtown San Francisco was a dream come true having (virtually and never literally) "designed" shows in that space while in graduate school under the tutelage of my mentor and fellow designer Ralph Funicello. It was commonplace in those days for Ralph to select a play and then select a theatre by bringing in drawings of the space.

Graduate design students like me marveled over the hand-drawn masterpieces that represented this historic space.

Just doing a *pretend* design in that theatre seemed like an honor of sorts! Built in 1906 it was, and still stands as, handcrafted elegance in the theatrical form but also boasts some amazing stage technology including a motorized raked stage. The theatre itself suffered catastrophic damage as a result of the

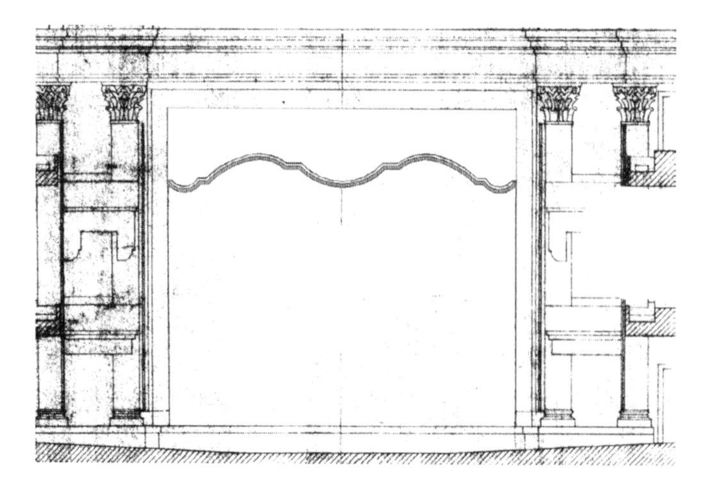

Figure 8.1 Front Elevation Drawing of American Conservatory Theatre (ACT)—San Francisco. *Source: ACT archives.*

Loma Prieta earthquake that struck San Francisco in 1989, which caused an air conditioning unit on the roof to crash through the coffered ceiling and crush the first five rows of the theatre, thankfully injuring no one.

The company was displaced for years, but the renovation gave the tenants an opportunity to update the space using concealed technology which rivaled any roadhouse in the city. The finished product gleamed with gold Corinthian columns and massive moldings. Designing in this space was like designing inside a Fabergé egg (see plate 20).

Figure 8.2 Photo of Post-Earthquake Geary Theatre in 1989. *Source: ACT archives.*

My second actualized design in that room was the play *A Moon for the Misbegotten* by Eugene O'Neill. After a success with my first show for ACT called *The Dazzle*, I was feeling confident that I could create something unique for the discerning audiences who chose to attend the play and live up to the reputation of the cast in the show. Thrilled to be working again with *Dazzle* director Laird Williamson, we pored over visual research in our first meeting, but Laird gravitated to a quote he had discovered in an early review of the play in 1944 by *Detroit News* journalist Russell McLaughlin.

Laird simply said: "I want the design to look like this quote."[8]

> His present characters, although they use some of the worst modern language ever heard on a stage, are actually dark, eerie, Celtic symbol-folk . . . who beat their breasts at the agony of living, battle titanically and drink like Nordic gods, but finally are seen to wear the garb of sainthood and die for love.[9]

The design evolved into a strikingly abstract iteration of the beloved play: on a raked stage exists a skeletal Connecticut farmhouse with a large collage of farmhouse architecture floating overhead—epic staging evocative of these epic characters and their language. Seven different gorgeous moons were projected on a rear-projection screen upstage with a sky gorgeously lit by the show's lighting designer, Don Darnutzer. A true demonstration of how a lighting designer/artist can "paint with light" (see plate 21).

Every aspect of the production performance by the actors and the design were lauded in the review by Steven Winn of the San Francisco Chronicle . . . except for the set design. What followed were phone calls from colleagues and friends all across the Bay area. An excerpt of the review discussing the design was as follows:

> Moon is a deceptively complicated play, with its threads of broad comedy, raw confession and moonlit transformation. Instead of providing a firmly articulated plane for the action, Robert Mark Morgan's regrettable set is a jumble of fussy, uncertain gestures and geometries. The Hogan farm shack's walls float overhead like some stylized fan. Fence lines scissor across the stage, and rocks are neatly gathered up, construction-site fashion.[10]

A review like that one felt so horrible at the time. It was not just the sting of the review that hurt, but the consistent feeling that I had failed the production and the team. My concern was that my design was a blemish on an otherwise stainless production, which deserved to be seen and appreciated. I have always been a fan of sports but have never felt so viscerally a sense of "letting down the team" on our stage.

> It is our failure to become our perceived ideal that ultimately defines us and makes us unique.
>
> Conan O'Brien[11]

Channel the Haters: Prove them Wrong

Artists and innovators are asked to "dare greatly" on a consistent basis. The sidelines are for the critics and, in the spirit of Frank Gehry staring down a journalist and responding to a comment about his work as "spectacle," there is nothing wrong with taking chances and experimenting with an idea. That idea might be a spatial volume as in a set design or literally *anything* else—

1. A painting, a play, or a poem.
2. A sonnet, a song, or a sculpture.
3. A chair, a cabin, or a character.
4. A book, a blog post, or brickwork.

Perhaps the greatest basketball player of all-time, Michael Jordan, used the doubters and the haters as fuel to drive himself to levels not seen in the sport prior to that point. He channeled all the negative reviews or premature declarations that he was "past his prime" into one determined and relentless force to train harder and play better than his previous game or his previous season. He relished the opportunity to show—with his talent—that the haters were all wrong about him. You've had those in your life as well. From the "Are you sure you want to do that?" to "Is there much of a future in that?" to the more blunt "Not sure you have it in you to (blank)." Spoken and unspoken, why not use the opposite of compliments and encouragement AS compliments and encouragement?

For the young artist, you must use negative comments by ANY critic as fuel for the fire. In the same way we can be moved and driven to succeed by encouragement from our peers, I feel far too often that we disregard what is a motivator in sports—the simple drive to prove someone wrong and not right.

9

Where Do We Go From Here?

Chapter Outline

The Certainty of Uncertainty

As I write this love-letter to designing, we in this merry band of "troubadours and minstrels" of the theatre are only at the beginning of realizing new possibilities for shared experiences. If the isolation of the pandemic has taught us anything, it is that we theatre artists *crave* convening. Others may be content with biding their time as introverts crafting art, but theatre artists are IN IT to craft art together. For some of us, it is the reason we do theatre AT ALL is to be in a room with other artists crafting a story together in this addictive collaborative artform known as theatre. And isolation was, and may still be, the antithesis to that artistic nourishment. Whether it be in a church or at a funeral, we long to mourn what we have lost together. Whether it be in a concert hall or a sports arena, we long to share an experience that involves equal parts excitement and pure joy. Those are lived experiences that teach us how to live . . . and we are collectively feeling the withdrawal. Mixed in with our many pandemic moments of isolation were a few glimmers and reminders of who we are as a human community. A kind word sent via email, a postcard from a far-flung friend, or a phone call from someone you have not spoken to in a great long time are a result of this collective disaster. The pause allowed a moment of reflection to assess and ponder who we are and where we are going. It has also allowed us a moment to discuss for whom we make the art and how we make it more accessible.

In the face of such loss, we must do what we do. We must create. We must make and contribute and prompt discussion somehow in new mediums.

> I'm always thinking about creating. My future starts when I wake up every morning . . . Every day I find something creative to do with my life.
>
> Miles Davis[1]

Take Stock: What has not Changed

What has *not* changed is who we are as *artists*. You are as talented now as you were pre-pandemic. Like Miles Davis, we are the only ones who have been there for *all* of our own performances. Take comfort in knowing that with the loss of so much else, there was no loss of talent. We have only paused from our creative making, but the time has come to begin again. Perhaps we take tentative steps into a new era of theatre, and art-making, and collaboration, and storytelling.

With that in mind, we need to put that talent to work and begin prototyping new volumes for new work. What is our new medium for sharing stories? What does a new space look like that allows us a real experience in a new way and on a new stage? How can it be fashioned and *designed* in way that allows for greater possibility than we had before? Beyond the liminal stage I described in the introduction, what new stage exists beyond the realm of in-person performance venues? Theatre has and will continue to survive as it has for centuries. Psychologists like to cite that past behavior of a patient is the best barometer for future behavior. If the theatre is a patient, it will certainly exist beyond the now and for eternity because of the basic human need for shared storytelling. What should the theatre of tomorrow *look* like if we are to continue with theatre into tomorrow?

We covered the If/Then exercise a little earlier: if this play we just read was an animal/color/person what kind of animal/color/person would it be?

We must ask that now of our entire artistic profession. With the same honest inquiry as those innocent if/then questions, we must ask ourselves "What should it look like?" when referring to the entire world of spoken word drama and including all the voices that contribute to making that a richer and more inclusive conversation. What does a virtual community *look* like? How global can storytelling get and maybe (just maybe) was our pandemic pause a way to envision something entirely new that forces the world to come together soaking-in and sharing in our commonality and community . . . virtually.

> Let's actually treasure the sense that we're right up against what we don't have, and therefore something new has to be created and imagined and invented and brought forth like a flower.
>
> Peter Sellars[2]

This unprecedented time has led to . . . well . . . time I have not had preceding this moment in history and that journey of discovery has been so fulfilling. In a gesture of collaboration as simple as a Google doc called *Theatre Without A Theatre,* I have been curating the many ways artists like ourselves are finding a way forward and approaching the great constraint of isolation as a catalyst for creativity. Since March of 2020, the document has grown to include over a hundred citations of what theatres and artists are doing all over the world to move the needle forward and find new volumes for storytelling.

> It is a time of confrontation, this transition, the time of transition of the old society to a new one that does not exist yet, but it's being created with the confrontation of the ghosts.
>
> Paulo Freire[3]

Re-think the Theatre Volume: Where are we . . . and Where is "Where"?

My own recent research and experiments pondering these questions have led me to potentially consider space in an entirely new way. Can space for both the design and the story told within it be virtual and does that open us up to greater possibility and connectivity? Might there be a way to create a model that IS the stage? Can a virtual environment actually open us up to possibilities and tools we did not have before? And can the design of an environment be as collaborative and fulfilling virtually as it has always been in person?

Channeling Morpheus from *The Matrix*, what if I told you that you could . . .

- Design a production as lavish as you wish without ever having to worry about cost?
- Teach students about design and have them pin-up their designs in a space that does not exist?
- See that design on stage without ever having to build it?
- Rehearse that production in real-time with ten actors in ten different locations around the globe?
- Produce that production in a theatre "space" where the rent, overhead costs, and equipment needs are non-existent.
- Invite a worldwide audience to that same production to experience storytelling on a global scale?

Spurred on by the combination of a need for increased access for audiences into experiences they cannot attend based on geographical or socioeconomic factors and technological advances in web-based XR platforms and spaces, a new frontier is opening up on the web that reveals a myriad of possibilities and opportunities for digital collaborators and storytellers in virtual venues that exist online. This new and exciting frontier asks that we question any assumptions that we have about designing and producing theatre from a pre-pandemic way of thinking. The tools for collaboration and storytelling are expanding by the moment. As we begin a new era, we can and should begin to think about inclusivity for theatre artists and patrons in a whole new world where the theatre "space" has a whole new definition and exists in an entirely new realm.

In one such example, I am working with colleagues in the Department of Earth & Planetary Sciences to explore using augmented reality (AR) as a tool for creating a classroom community online as they develop and test an app that allows students to see geological objects and structures in augmented reality. In one click, a student can place something as tiny as a crystal lattice structure or as large as an Apollo landing site on the surface of the moon on a kitchen table. In this medium, they can truly explore it and respond to it spinning it around as needed and viewing it from all different angles. This discovery naturally led me to the beginning of a "what if . . ." What if my students could (virtually) gather around a student model that would allow us to respond to it and discuss it together in much the same way students do in any in-person studio class? (See plate 22.) In this scenario, we replace matte board and glue with a computer model and the "classroom" becomes many rooms where the virtual model may be placed in an AR way. For ten students, a model may be placed on ten different tables in ten different places around the world. The space has changed, but the normal and necessary act of discussing that space and the design within it in a classroom setting does not. The experience can allow us the possibility of swooping into the model like a boom shot on a movie set and exploring the room and the stage design from all different kinds of viewpoints: that of the actor, of the audience, even of the backstage crew. We are **in** it. In a way we have not been before. What possibilities can we create with this type of technology at our disposal?

A group of coders online with a directive from a virtual co-working platform called VirBela are exploring these limits right now. They have created an online venue with multiple environments called FrameVR. Each space can have an individuality of look that we designers crave. The result is a virtual venue with a cost of access at zero. A visitor can design their own avatar, enter the space, and engage with colleagues and friends in a way that seems as organic as a real-life conversation. In that venue, creators have access to tools that can make the space anything from a product launch to a space to critique student projects (see plate 23).

To test the platform, I recruited two students who had a pre-rehearsed scene from a play perform that scene in a Web XR environment in Frame. We setup an outdoor theatre space inside of a 360° panoramic photo of our university campus and invited colleagues and students to join us for a "virtual theatre experiment" on a Thursday night. After the performance, we had a post-show talkback (as we do sometimes in a real theatre) to discuss impressions and whether this new method of storytelling could work for virtual performance. Many acting/directing colleagues were genuinely concerned about the (virtual) actor's capacity to express emotion as an avatar with no arms, legs, or, perhaps more importantly, facial expressions. Completely valid! However, it is important to remind ourselves that this type of technology and the democratization of this type of storytelling is only in its infancy. Strides can and continue to be made. In fact, advancements have likely been made since you began reading this paragraph.

As I learned with the *Avatar* exhibition I designed in 2010, James Cameron was quick to underline the need for the technology he was using to create the film to not simply motion capture, but *performance* capture. Assembling actors in an aircraft hangar in Santa Monica to shoot the film, he wanted their performance and facial expressions to shine through whether they were portraying themselves as a human or a ten-foot-tall Na'vi character in the film. That humanity, despite the layers and layers of computer-generated filters, underscored the need for an audience (all of us) to see ourselves as those characters and share in a common humanity and empathy with them.

WebXR platforms are rapidly advancing towards a common humanity in the spirit of *Avatar* performances. It is only a matter of time. Creative teams for productions now online may include not only designers familiar with working together in an in-person realm but may also loop in artists who work in film, video production, computer graphics, etc. offering up new viewpoints on a story that launch new endeavors into new online territories with a worldwide cast and audience. With these new storytellers, what kind of stories can we tell? … and to whom? … and for whom?

Like David Lynch's bait on the hook example of idea-making, ideas (and the technology to support them) keep flowing. "What if …" Once designed to suit our story, whatever it may be, can a designer's computer model actually **BE** the stage and not merely a representation of a stage? Unencumbered by the usual discussions and concessions related to production costs, are we now entering a new frontier in a virtual realm where we designers can have absolutely anything we can dream up—a castle, an island, a city—simply dropped into a virtual realm? Using virtual reality, can the space we create actually **BE** the space where the performance takes place? And if that is the case, who are the "actors" and how do we transport them there? How does an audience witness it together and can we experience a story well told again … *together*. We are on the precipice with a foot in two realms: one foot in the possible with new tools and worlds at our disposal and one firmly planted in *story*: what we know works and what we hope to recreate in a new space.

For more live theatre outdoors, how about the live theatrical equivalent of a drive-in movie? Designer Emanuele Sinisi proposed a circular performance venue lit by car headlights and LA-based choreographer Jacob Jonas used the idea to stage dance during a pandemic (see plate 24).

And the Pageant Wagon first introduced in the introduction to this text? Yes—it happened as well! (See plate 25.)

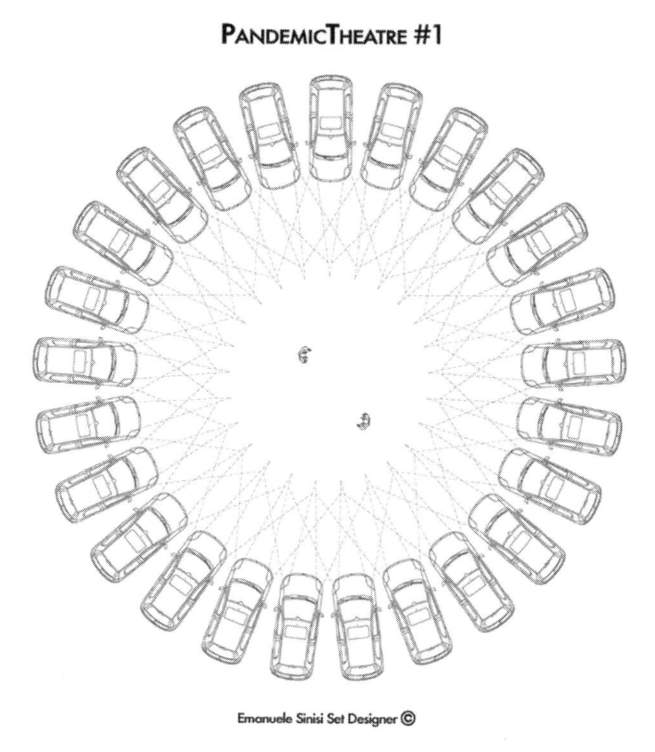

Figure 9.1 Design for Pandemic Theatre by Designer Emanuele Sinisi. *Source: permission granted by Designer Emanuele Sinisi*

Don't Box Up Your Artistic Shop!

With all this uncertainty comes possibility for new venues and new forms of artistic expression. This is not the time to pack up shop and wait out a pandemic until we return to "normal." This is a time to explore breaking out of our interior spaces and into new ones outdoors and in virtual environments!

I do not have all the answers, but I would like to think that I've got a lot of ideas to prototype and try on the theatre-going public, largely believed to be the most understanding of audiences of any kind. An earlier reference to the adventurous souls that occupy both volumes in front of and behind the curtain should certainly be willing to go on a journey with us if we propose a new way for community storytelling. This is not the end, but a new beginning. And the foot-soldiers of our new artistic inventions are us collaborating with each other in a new realm of theatre with new constraints, but also unburdened by the expectations of old. Perhaps one day the mere idea that we got dressed up to attend a performance accessible to only a fraction of our fellow humans will be as foreign and unknown to us as our collective theatrical future is to us now. What's past is prologue. And what comes next is up to us!

> When the artist is alive in any person, whatever his kind of work may be, he becomes an inventive, searching, daring, self-expressing creature. He becomes interesting to other people. He disturbs, upsets, enlightens, and he opens ways for a better understanding. Where those who are not artists are trying to close the book, he opens it, shows there are still more pages possible.
>
> Robert Henri[4]

Notes

Introduction: . . . "And Just Like That"

1. Joan Didion, "The White Album," in *We Tell Ourselves Stories in Order to Live*, (New York: Alfred A. Knopf, 2006), 185.
2. Lorinda Mamo, "Design and Story," *A Bird with a French Fry*, May 29, 2016. Available at: https://abirdwithafrenchfry.com/design-and-story/.
3. Frank Gehry, *Sketches of Frank Gehry*, directed by Sydney Pollack (Hollywood: Sony Pictures Classics, 2006).
4. Buckminster Fuller, *A Fuller View: Buckminster Fuller's Vision of Hope and Abundance for All* by L. Steven Sieden (Nederland, CO: Divine Arts, 2011), 256
5. Rebecca Solnit, "A Tale of Two Princes: The Halifax Explosion and After," in *A Paradise Built in Hell,* (New York: Penguin Publishing Group, 2009), 95.
6. Jessica Helfand, "Canoeing," The Self-Reliance Project, *Design Observer,* April 6, 2020. Available at: https://designobserver.com/feature/canoeing/40214.
7. John Steinbeck, *Once There Was a War,* (New York: Penguin Books, 1997), 23.

1 The Designer as A Child Futurist

1. Twyla Tharp, *The Creative Habit*, (New York: Simon and Schuster, 2003), 75–77.
2. Bruce Rogers, "Design as Change Agent: Interview with Brian Collins," *Forbes*, May 4, 2019. Available at: www.forbes.com/sites/brucerogers/2019/03/04/design-as-change-agent-interview-with-brian-collins/?sh=3af57cb14e27.
3. Albert Einstein (letter to his friend, Otto Juliusburger, September 1942), *The Ultimate Quotable Einstein*, (Princeton, NJ: Princeton University Press, 2011), 55–56.

4. Tharp, *The Creative Habit.*
5. Sir Ken Robinson, "Do schools kill creativity?" February 2006, TED video, 19:12. Available at: www.ted.com/talks/sir_ken_robinson_do_schools_kill_creativity.
6. Pablo Picasso, quoted in Ken Robinson, "Do schools kill creativity?"
7. Richard Pascale, *The Power of Positive Deviance: How Unlikely Innovators Solve the World's Toughest Problems*, (Cambridge, MA: Harvard Business Review Press, 2010).
8. Robert Edmond Jones, *The Dramatic Imagination*, (New York, NY: Theatre Arts Books, 1941), 42.
9. Federico Garcia Lorca, *Only Mystery: Federico Garcia Lorca's Poetry in Word and Image*, (Gainesville, FL: University Press of Florida, 1992).
10. Howard Rheingold (@hrheingold), "Many calls themselves 'futurists'— Bryan actually knows how to do it," Twitter, January 15, 2020, 1:23 p.m. Available at: https://twitter.com/hrheingold/status/1217527663121686528?s=20.
11. Oskar Eustis, "Why theatre is essential to democracy" 2018, TED video, 13:01. Available at: www.ted.com/talks/oskar_eustis_why_theatre_is_essential_to_democracy/transcript?language=en.
12. Randy Pausch, "The Last Lecture: Achieving Your Childhood Dreams" December 2007, Carnegie Mellon University https://youtu.be/ji5_MqicxSo.
13. Pantelis Dessyllas, *Opera* edited by Rudolf Hartmann, (New York, NY: William Morrow & Co, Inc, 1977), 76–77.
14. Wendy Kesselman, *The Diary of Anne Frank,* (New York, NY: Dramatists Play Service, January 1, 1998).

2 Empathy and Answering, "What Story Are We Telling?" with Collaborators

1. Sir Ken Robinson, "Imagination and Empathy" November 2011, Dalai Lama Center for Peace and Education, 0:25. Available at: www.youtube.com/watch?v=Yu2zcmb3yAQ
2. Robert Edmond Jones, *The Dramatic Imagination*, (New York, NY: Theatre Arts Books, 1941), 31.
3. William Shakespeare, *Hamlet,* Act I, Scene 3. OpenSource Shakespeare. Available at: www.opensource Shakespeare.org.
4. William Shakespeare, *Hamlet,* Act I, Scene 4. OpenSource Shakespeare. Available at: www.opensource Shakespeare.org.

5. William Shakespeare, *Richard III*, Act I, Scene 1, lines 39–40. OpenSource Shakespeare. Available at: www.opensource Shakespeare.org.
6. Albert Einstein, *The Ultimate Quotable Einstein*, (Princeton, NJ: Princeton University Press, 2011)

3 The Importance of Research as "Fuel" for ANY Process

1. Michael Webber, *Signature Course Stories*, (Austin, TX: University of Texas Press, 2015): 105.
2. Shakespeare, *Hamlet*, Act I, Scene 2, lines 180–185. OpenSource Shakespeare. Available at: www.opensource Shakespeare.org.
3. Wikipedia, "Circle," accessed June 7, 2021. Available at: https://en.wikipedia.org/wiki/Circle.
4. Anne Trafton, "In the blink of an eye" January 16, 2014. Available at: https://news.mit.edu/2014/in-the-blink-of-an-eye-0116
5. Dorotea Kovacevic, Maja Brozovic, & Klementia Mozina "Improving visual search in instruction manuals using pictograms" February 2016, Available at: www.researchgate.net/publication/294723381_Improving_visual_search_in_instruction_manuals_using_pictograms
6. Idris Mootee, "10 Design Thinking Principles for Business and Strategy Innovation" (PowerPoint, Idea Couture Inc., Nov. 22, 2007). Available at: www.slideshare.net/imootee/innovation-and-design-thinking-idris-mootee
7. Bill Parcells to Tony Romo, overheard on football broadcast
8. Robert Benchley, *Of All Things*, (New York: Henry Holt and Company, 1921): 187.
9. Patricia Zipprodt, conversation with the author.

4 Clawing and Scratching Out an Idea

1. Bruce Mau, "Incomplete Manifesto for Growth," Massive Change Network, #4. Available at: www.massivechangenetwork.com/bruce-mau-manifesto.
2. Ibid., #6.
3. Ibid., #15.

4. Bruce Mau, "Bruce Mau On: What is the Centre for Massive Change" January 2010, 2:39. Available at: https://youtu.be/XpRxAovJM7g.
5. Leonard Cohen, "Leonard Cohen Offers Rare Peek into His Process at 'Popular Problems' Preview," interviewed by Steve Appleford, *RollingStone Magazine*, September 11, 2015. Available at: www.rollingstone.com/music/music-live-reviews/leonard-cohen-offers-rare-peek-into-his-process-at-popular-problems-preview-76635/.
6. Frank Gehry, *Sketches of Frank Gehry*. American Masters, PBS.
7. Mihaly Csikszentmihalyi, *Flow: The Psychology of Optimal Experience*, (New York, NY: Harper Perennial Modern Classics; 1st edition, 2008)
8. Joy Paul Guilford, Alternative Uses Test from Creative Huddle. Available at: www.creativehuddle.co.uk/post/the-alternative-uses-test.
9. Burt Rutan, quoted in Peter Diamandis, " TRUE BREAKTHROUGHS = CRAZY IDEAS + PASSION," Peter H. Diamandis, May 21, 2017. Available at: www.diamandis.com/blog/true-breakthroughs-crazy-ideas-passion
10. Kato Buss, "Imagination and Empathy: the Call of the Clown," November 20, 2015, TedXUco Video, 11:03. Available at: www.youtube.com/watch?v=BlkPppKZajM.
11. Ibid.
12. Francis Bacon from interview with David Sylvester, October 1962. Available at: https://theoria.art-zoo.com/interview-with-david-sylvester-francis-bacon/.
13. Ming Cho Lee, overheard by author
14. Elizabeth Gilbert, "Your elusive creative genius." TED Talk. Available at: www.ted.com/talks/elizabeth_gilbert_your_elusive_creative_genius.
15. Marcus E. Raichle, "A default mode to brain function", Proceedings of the National Academy of Sciences of the United States of America (PNAS), January 2001. Available at: www.pnas.org/content/98/2/676.

5 Modeling and Shaping an Object and an Idea

1. Franklin D. Roosevelt, Wiktionary. Available at: https://en.wiktionary.org/wiki/a_smooth_sea_never_made_a_skilled_sailor;
2. Thomas Edison, *Edison: His Life and Inventions* by Frank Lewis Dyer and Thomas Commerford Martin from story by Edison associate Walter S. Mallory, 1910
3. Frank Gehry, Sketches of Frank Gehry, American Masters, PBS.
4. Ibid.

5. Tom & David Kelley, *Creative Confidence: Unleashing the Creative Potential Within Us All*, (London, UK: William Collins, an imprint of HarperCollins Publishers, 2013): 137
6. Agnes De Mille, *Martha: The Life and Work of Martha Graham—A Biography* (New York: Random House, 1991).

6 Creative Swings, Career Fields, and Collaboration

1. Charles Mitchell and David Learmond, *Go Where There Be Dragons: Leadership Essentials for 2020 and Beyond*, (Council Perspectives by the Conference Board, 2010): 4
2. John Carver Sullivan, conversation with author.
3. Thomas Merton, *Thomas Merton: Selected Essays* (Maryknoll, NY: Orbis Books, 2013): pp. 232–239. Used with Permission of the Merton Legacy Trust.
4. Ellen Winner, *Gifted Children: Myths and Realities* (New York, NY: Basic Books, 1996)
5. Merriam Webster, "Misfit", accessed June 7, 2021. Available at: www.merriam-webster.com/dictionary/misfit.
6. Walt Whitman, "By the Roadside," in *Leaves of Grass,* 6th Edition, (Philadelphia: David McKay, 1891), 215.
7. Orville Wright, "The Wright Brothers' Aeroplane," *Century Magazine*, September 1908. Available at: www.loc.gov/item/wright003333/.
8. Brian Uzzi and Jarrett Spiro, "Collaboration and Creativity: The Small World Problem," *AJS* 111, no. 2 (2005). Available at: www.kellogg.northwestern.edu/faculty/uzzi/ftp/uzzi%27s_research_papers/0900904.pdf.
9. Ibid., 7.
10. Ibid., 16–18.
11. Wikipedia, "Groupthink", accessed June 7, 2021. Available at: https://en.wikipedia.org/wiki/Groupthink.

7 The Tech and Preview Process—the Ultimate Proof-of-Concept

1. Michael Ganio, conversation with author.
2. Marle Anne Chiment, conversation with author.
3. Ibid.

4. George Bernard Shaw, *Major Barbara*, (New York: Brentanos, 1917), 143.
5. Ibid., 70.
6. Ibid., 133.
7. Ibid., 143.

8 The Inevitability of Failure and the Sea of Criticism

1. Paco Tolson (@pacotolson), "The business of #theatre demands you have a completely fortified heart . . ." Twitter, August 15, 2019, 2:10 p.m. Available at: https://twitter.com/pacotolson/status/1162079174783188992?s=20.
2. Theodore Roosevelt, "Citizenship in a Republic" (speech, April 23, 1910, Paris), Theodore Roosevelt Center. Available at: www.theodorerooseveltcenter.org/Learn-About-TR/TR-Encyclopedia/Culture-and-Society/Man-in-the-Arena.aspx.
3. Janet Rae-Dupree Let Computers Compute. It's the Age of the Right Brain. The New York Times. Available at: /www.nytimes.com/2008/04/06/technology/06unbox.html .
4. Gehry, *Sketches of Frank Gehry*. American Masters, PBS.
5. Ibid
6. Ibid
7. Julius Meier-Graefe, *The Formation of a Legend: Van Gogh Criticism 1890–1920*, (Ann Arbor, MI: UMI Research Press, 1980), 113
8. Laird Williamson, conversation with author.
9. Laura Shea, "O'Neill, the Theatre Guild, and 'A Moon for the Misbegotten'", *The Eugene O'Neill Review*, 2005, Vol 27 (2005): 87
10. Steven Winn, "Nimble pas de deux sparks ACT's just-right reading of O'Neill's 'Moon'", *San Francisco Chronicle*, May 6, 2005. Available at: www.sfgate.com/entertainment/article/THEATRE-REVIEWS-Nimble-pas-de-deux-sparks-ACT-s-2349292.php.
11. Conan O'Brien, "2011 Dartmouth College Commencement Address," (speech, New Hampshire, 2011). Available at: www.youtube.com/watch?v=KmDYXaaT9sA.

9 Where Do We Go From Here?

1. Miles Davis, *Miles* (New York: Simon and Schuster, 1990).
2. Peter Sellars, "Can artists find a silver lining in the cloud of COVID-19? Peter Sellars is looking," interview by Mark Swed, *LA Times*, April 11,

2020. Available at: www.latimes.com/entertainment-arts/story/2020-04-11 /coronavirus-pandemic-peter-sellars.

3. Paulo Friere, *Pedagogy of the Oppressed*, (New York, NY: Continuum International Publishing Group Inc, 1970).
4. Robert Henri, *The Art Spirit : Notes, Articles, Fragments of Letters and Talks to Students, Bearing on the Concept and Technique of Picture Making, the Study of Art Generally, and on Appreciation* (Philadelphia: J.B. Lippincott, 1923): 11.

Further Reading

Arnold Aronson, *American Set Design* (New York: Theatre Communications Group, 1993).

Stephen Di Benedetto, *An Introduction to Theatre Design* (London: Routledge, 2012).

David Epstein, *Range: Why Generalists Triumph in a Specialized World* (New York: Riverhead Books; Illustrated Edition, 2019).

Robert Edmond Jones, *The Dramatic Imagination: Reflections and Speculations on the Art of the Theatre* (New York: Routledge, 2004).

David & Tom Kelley, *Creative Confidence: Unleashing the Creative Potential Within Us All* (New York: Crown Publishing Group, 2013).

James Moody, *The Business of Theatrical Design* Second Edition (New York: Allworth Press, 2013).

Lynn Pecktal, *Designing and Painting for the Theatre* Third Edition (New York: Holt, Rinehart, and Winston, 1975).

Twyla Tharp, *The Creative Habit: Learn It And Use It For Life* (New York: Simon & Schuster, 2006).

Index